Table of Contents

Unit 1	Introduction	1
Unit 2	Coding for Physician's Services	3
Unit 3	Life Cycle of a Claim	19
Unit 4	Completing the CMS-1500 Claim Form	35
Unit 5	Completing the UB-04 Claim Form	53
Unit 6	Reimbursement Methodologies	71
Unit 7	Quality Assurance Practices and Regulatory Compliance	111
Unit 8	Diagnostic Related Groups	123
	Answer Key	137
	Appendix	149

Exploring Healthcare Reimbursement

Career Step, LLC
Phone: 801.489.9393
Toll-Free: 800.246.7837
Fax: 801.491.6645
careerstep.com

This text companion contains a snapshot of the online program content converted to a printed format. Please note that the online training program is constantly changing and improving and is always the source of the most up-to-date information.

Product Number: HG-PR-11-038
Generation Date: April 20, 2011

© Career Step - All Rights Reserved.
The material in this book may not be copied or distributed without express written consent from Career Step.

Unit 1
Introduction

Introduction to Exploring Healthcare Reimbursement

Exploring Healthcare Reimbursement

This module provides detailed information about the various types of payment systems used to reimburse inpatient and outpatient medical services. Additionally, the module introduces information about claims processing, coding, billing, auditing, diagnostic related groups, and monitoring the coding process.

Getting paid for providing services is what healthcare reimbursement is all about. A healthcare provider (individual or institution) performs a healthcare service for a patient and receives payment in return for the service. Building on what you learned in prior modules about healthcare documentation, structure, and organization, let's take a look at healthcare reimbursement.

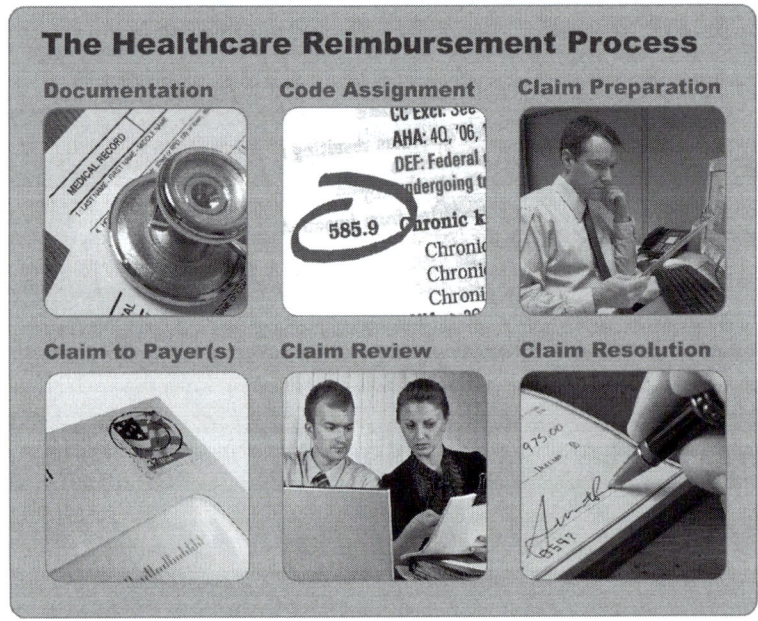

Regardless of who pays the claim, the healthcare reimbursement process has the same basic elements:

1. documentation – medical record/financial record
2. code assignment
3. claim preparation
4. claim to payer(s)
5. claim review
6. claim resolution

The details, such as how much is billed, how much is paid, and what forms are used, may vary from claim to claim, but the billing process is the same for all healthcare services.

Medical Humor

"The doctor said he would have me on my feet in two weeks."

"And did he?"

"Yes. I had to sell my car to pay the bill."

2

Unit 2
Coding for Physician's Services

Coding for Physician's Services – Introduction

Okay, let's start by delving into coding and billing for different outpatient settings.

We are going to examine closely the basics of coding and healthcare reimbursement for physicians. From a medical coding specialist's perspective, there are two types of outpatient coding situations: coding for physicians and coding for facilities. We'll take a look at both, since you never know if your career might take you down the path of a physician's office or a facility.

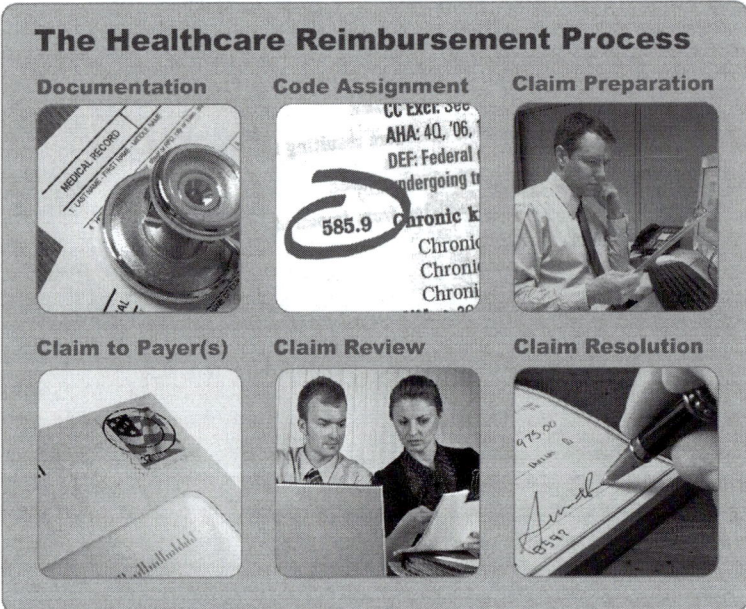

Coding at the Physician's Office

Physicians' offices, whether a single physician or a group of physicians, are a special case for coding and billing. When a physician provides care in an office where the physician owns the equipment and facility, the professional services of the physician and the equipment and supply charges are bundled together and billed on a CMS-1500 form. For the purposes of third-party payers, the services of the physician and the facility are included in the CPT® codes chosen when the physician provides care at his/her own office.

When a patient is seen at a physician's office or receives care in a physician's clinic, the billing and coding process is as follows:

> **Coding/Billing for Healthcare Services at Physician's Office**
>
> - *Diagnosis Codes – ICD-9-CM Volumes I and II*
> - *Procedure Codes – CPT®*
> - *Supply Codes – HCPCS (if applicable)*
> - *Billing – CMS-1500 form*

Physician offices can range from small, single physician offices to large, multiple physician clinics with laboratory, radiology, and minor surgery capabilities. The size of the office does not matter for the purposes of the medical coder. Care received in the physician office where the physician or physician group owns the facility is always coded with the diagnosis code from ICD-9-CM Volumes I and II and procedures from the CPT® codebook.

> We've placed a visual aid in the appendix on page 150.
>
> We've placed a visual aid in the appendix on page 151.

I. **TRUE/FALSE.**
   Mark the following true or false.

   1. Physician's offices only use the CMS-1500 form for billing.
      - ● true
      - ○ false

   2. The billing and coding process at a physician's clinic begins with procedure codes from CPT.
      - ○ true
      - ● false

   3. A large physician's office will have a different billing procedure than a small one.
      - ○ true
      - ● false

Physician Care at Outside Facilities

In addition to physicians providing care in the office setting, medical coders who work for physicians or physician groups will also code the physician's services performed outside the physician's office. A physician who sees patients in the office also will have privileges at independent healthcare facilities, such as hospitals, nursing homes, or convalescent homes. When a physician sees a patient in one of those settings, the professional services are coded and billed by the physician's staff and not by the hospital, nursing home, or convalescent home. The medical coding specialist and medical biller for the physician will code and bill for the patient's care as follows:

Highlights

Occasionally a physician will take supplies when visiting patients at an outside facility to provide patient care. Those supplies are coded and billed by the physician's support staff.

Coding/Billing for Healthcare Services at an Independent Facility

- *Diagnosis Codes – ICD-9-CM Volumes I and II*
- *Procedure Codes – CPT®*
- *Supply Codes – HCPCS LEVEL II (if applicable)*
- *Billing – CMS-1500 form*

Physicians will sometimes take supplies with them when visiting an outpatient facility to provide care. For example, a podiatrist doing a foot clinic in a nursing home may bring his own instruments and dressings for providing podiatric care. Or an orthopedist visiting a patient in a convalescent home may bring a supply of needles and medicines to perform joint injections or other orthopedic care services. In these cases, the supplies provided by the physician are coded and billed by the physician's healthcare support staff on the CMS-1500.

We've placed a visual aid in the appendix on page 152.

I. **TRUE/FALSE.**
   Mark the following true or false.

   1. A physician who sees patients in outside facilities will have the services coded by his or her own staff.
      - ● true
      - ○ false

   2. The physician's staff will use only a CMS-1500 form when billing for his or her work at an outside facility.
      - ● true
      - ○ false

   3. If a physician brings supplies with him when visiting an outpatient facility, it is billed on a UB-04.
      - ○ true
      - ● false

Healthcare Providers at Outside Facilities

Medical coders and billers may also be employed by less "traditional" physicians or physicians' groups, such as radiologists or emergency room physicians. These professional healthcare providers don't generally have a physical office where they see patients; instead the physicians contract to provide professional services at independent healthcare providers (institutions).

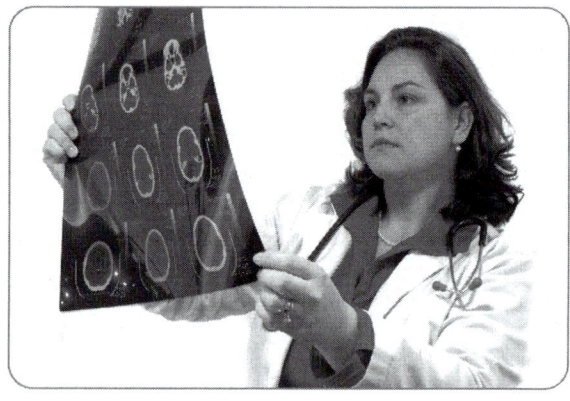

When a patient receives professional services at a standalone or independent healthcare facility, such as a hospital, radiology clinic, or independent laboratory, the professional services are coded and billed by the physician's staff and not by the hospital, radiology clinic, or independent facility. The medical coding specialist and medical biller for the physician/physicians' group will code and bill the professional services for the patient's healthcare.

We've placed a visual aid in the appendix on page 153.

Coding/Billing for Physician Services at Independent Facility

- *Diagnosis Codes – ICD-9-CM Volumes I and II*
- *Procedure Codes – CPT®*
- *Supply Codes – HCPCS (if applicable)*
- *Billing – CMS-1500 form*

Don't be fooled by the term "sees patient." The physician does not always have to see the patient. Every now and then, a patient will receive professional services without ever seeing the physician providing the services. Radiologists and pathologists are good examples of this type of professional care. Radiologists and pathologists rarely have an office where patients go to be seen. More often, radiologists and pathologists form a physician group that provides professional services—reading radiologic tests or examining tissue—for patients seen in an independent facility. In many cases, the radiologist or pathologist sees only the films or the tissue specimen and not the whole patient.

The medical coding and medical billing for radiology professional services falls under the same coding and billing pattern as other physician-based medical coding and billing. However, these types of professionals rarely, if ever, have supplies to be coded.

> We've placed a visual aid in the appendix on page 154.

Coding/Billing for Physician Professional Services

- *Diagnosis Codes – ICD–9–CM Volumes I and II*
- *Procedure Codes – CPT®*
- *Billing – CMS-1500 form*

Other Non-Physician Professionals

Individual healthcare service provider coding and billing does not always center around physician-based care. Some of you will have the opportunity to work in mental health or other specialized areas where psychologists, physical therapists, counselors, or other provider professional services are coded and billed. Regardless of whether or not the provider is a licensed social worker, physical therapist, physician, nurse practitioner, or physician's assistant, the same rules apply to coding and billing for healthcare services. This applies even when the professional providers are providing services in their offices or at independent facilities.

> We've placed a visual aid in the appendix on page 155.

Coding/Billing for Non-Physician Professional Services at Independent Facility

- *Diagnosis Codes – ICD-9-CM Volumes I and II*
- *Procedure Codes – CPT®*
- *Supply Codes – HCPCS (if applicable)*
- *Billing – CMS-1500 form*

Remember, non-physician professional service providers (with very few exceptions) provide services under the direction of a physician. For review, see Healthcare Providers – Individual in the Healthcare Structure and Organization module.

Review: Coding for Physicians

I. **TRUE/FALSE.**
   Mark the following true or false.

   1. Volumes 1, 2, and 3 in the ICD-9-CM codebook are used in the coding and billing process for professional services.
      - ○ true
      - ● false

   2. The professional services performed by a physician are billed on the CMS-1500 claim form.
      - ● true
      - ○ false

   3. Procedures performed at a physician's office are reported with CPT® codes.
      - ● true
      - ○ false

   4. The coding and billing of non-physician professional services are coded and billed differently than physician professional services.
      - ○ true
      - ● false

   5. When physicians provide their own supplies while visiting an outpatient facility to provide care, they can code and bill for these supplies.
      - ● true
      - ○ false

Coding for Facilities

When the physician provides patient care in the office or clinic, the equipment, supplies, and facility charges are coded and billed on the CMS-1500 and coded and billed by healthcare support staff employed by the physician or physicians' group. Professional services (physician charges) for patients seen in independent or standalone healthcare facilities are also coded and billed by coders and billers employed by the physician or physicians' group.

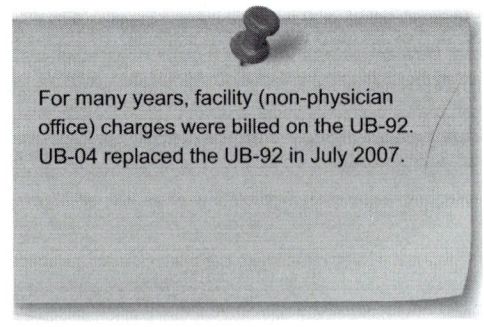

For many years, facility (non-physician office) charges were billed on the UB-92. UB-04 replaced the UB-92 in July 2007.

The other coding and billing opportunity is coding and billing for facilities providing healthcare setting only, not owned by the physician or physicians' group. Hospitals, surgery centers, urgent care centers, standalone radiology clinics, nursing homes, convalescent homes, and other inpatient and outpatient facilities employ healthcare support staff to handle coding and billing for the use of facility, equipment, supplies, and other costs associated with providing outpatient healthcare services. These facility charges are billed on the UB-04.

Medical coding and billing for facilities providing institutional outpatient services is as follows:

Coding/Billing for Healthcare Institutions

- *Diagnosis Codes – ICD-9-CM Volumes I and II*
- *Procedure Codes – CPT® (billing)*
  ICD-9 Volume III (facility tracking)
- *Supply Codes – HCPCS (as appropriate)*
- *Billing – UB-04 form*

> **Highlights**
>
> ICD-9-CM Volume III procedure coding is a common practice for facilities but these codes are NOT used for billing. ICD-9-CM procedure coding for outpatient services is strictly for the facility to track services rendered.

Notice the addition of the ICD-9-CM Volume III procedure coding for outpatient facilities. ICD-9-CM Volume III procedure coding is a common practice for facilities but these codes are **not** used for billing. ICD-9-CM procedure coding for outpatient services is strictly for the facility to track services rendered. When submitting a claim to a third-party payer for reimbursement, a medical biller would not use an ICD-9-CM procedure code.

> We've placed a visual aid in the appendix on page 156.

The Medicare Exception

You know, of course, there will be exceptions to every rule. Big sigh! But fortunately the exceptions for medical coders are not too onerous in the outpatient setting. When a medical coder is working for an ambulatory surgical center (also known as same-day surgery), the coding and billing requirements are different if the patient receiving care has third-party coverage through Medicare. Medicare requires all charges for same-day surgery to be billed on the CMS-1500. Medicare will still receive two separate bills; one bill for professional services from the physician on the CMS-1500 and the other for the facility, supply, and equipment charges from the ambulatory surgical center from the outpatient facility (also on the CMS-1500). Therefore, the coding and billing process for the ambulatory surgical center for Medicare patients is as follows:

> We've placed a visual aid in the appendix on page 157.

Coding/Billing for Medicare Patients for Outpatient Surgery

- *Diagnosis Codes – ICD-9 Volumes I and II*
- *Procedure Codes – CPT® (billing)*
  ICD-9 Volume III (facility tracking)
- *Supply Codes – HCPCS (as appropriate)*
- *Billing – CMS-1500*

Outpatient Coding by Service Provider

CMS-1500	UB-04

Physician Office
 	
Physician Professional Services
 	
Outpatient (Ambulatory/Same-Day) Surgery for Medicare Patients
	Healthcare Institutions (Non-Physician Office)
	
	    Hospital Outpatient
	    Radiology
	    Emergency Room
	    Nursing Home
	    Ambulatory Surgery
	    Urgent Care Clinics
	    Mental Health Clinics
	    Convalescent Homes
	    And all other OP providers

Coding Process	**Coding Process**
Diagnosis Codes: - ICD-9 Volumes I and II Procedures Codes: - CPT® Supply Codes: - HCPCS	Diagnosis Codes: - ICD-9 Volumes I and II Procedures Codes: - CPT (billing) and ICD-9 - Volume III (tracking) Supply Codes: - HCPCS

Certain specialties may require additional codes for third-party payers and/or disease or procedure tracking. For example, mental health and oncology have specialty coding books: *Diagnostic and Statistical Manual of Mental Disorders – DSM-IV-TR* and *ASTRO* or *ACR Guide to Radiation Oncology Coding 2007*. If you find yourself employed in a specialty setting when you move from graduation to employment, your employer will make you aware of any specialty coding requirements they may have.

Review: Coding for Facilities

I. **TRUE/FALSE.**
   Mark the following true or false.

   1. Emergency room services are billed on the UB-04 claim form.
      - ● true
      - ○ false

   2. All facility charges are reported on the UB-04 claim form.
      - ○ true
      - ● false

3. Facility charges are billed on the CMS-1500 claim form.
   - ○ true
   - ● false

4. ICD-9-CM procedure codes for outpatient services are used only by the facility to track the services rendered and not to determine reimbursement.
   - ● true
   - ○ false

5. The charges for Medicare patients seen in an ambulatory surgical center are billed on the CMS-1500 claim form.
   - ● true
   - ○ false

Outpatient Billing Process

In many cases, the medical coder is also the medical biller. In situations where this is not the case, the medical billing specialist and the medical coding specialist work closely together during the healthcare reimbursement process. As the patient is seen in the outpatient setting, the information is compiled and at the conclusion of the visit it is routed to the medical billing specialist.

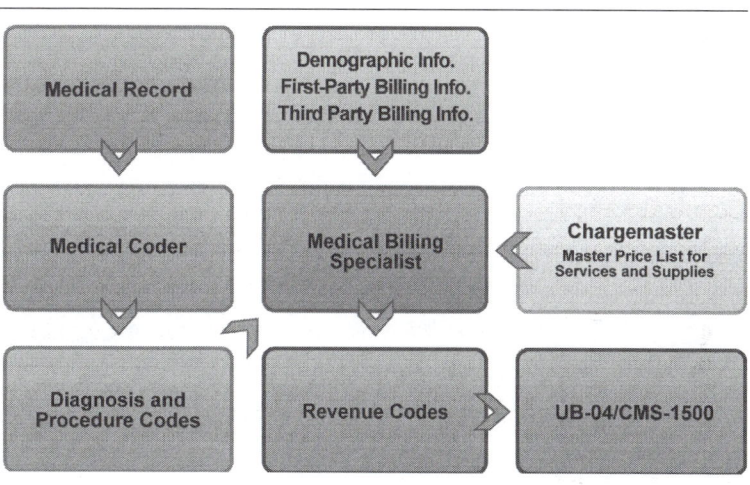

Demographic Information

Collection of demographic information is a standard part of the healthcare documentation process and is essential for the healthcare reimbursement process. The medical biller uses the demographic information as the foundation for determining who should receive the bill(s) and who has responsibility for payment.

Demographic information is collected by the front office either during a pre-registration or registration for patient care process. Demographic information may be collected by a front office staff person who then goes on to do the coding and billing for each patient in a physician's office or small clinic. Demographic information may also be done by an admissions or registration department collecting demographic information for all patient care services throughout a large multi-use facility. The people who collect the demographic information in an acute care hospital admission area, for example, would likely never see the coded medical record or the bills generated.

Coding and billing specialists for radiologists, emergency room physicians, or other patient care providers are likely to receive demographic information secondhand through the facility where the patient received the services.

Accurate Demographics

Collecting accurate and complete demographic information makes the billing process go more smoothly and is an important part of maintaining a financially healthy business. When the time from service to payment is stretched out because of bad demographic information (such as returned mail from a bad address or inaccurate third-party payer information on a CMS-1500 or UB-04), a provider can experience cash flow problems. When most claims are paid in a timely manner because patient contact information, third-party payer information, and other demographic information is accurately collected up front, a provider can more easily absorb the bad debts and occasional denials that are an inevitable part of doing business.

Demographics include some or all of the following:

- Patient name
- Patient date of birth
- Patient address
- Patient phone number
- Patient e-mail address
- Patient social security number
- Patient's employer
- Employer's phone number
- Spouse's name (if patient is married)
- Spouse's date of birth
- Spouse's phone number (other than home)
- Responsible party name
- Responsible party address (if different from patient)
- Responsible party phone number
- Emergency contact name
- Emergency contact number
- Third-party payer name
- Third-party payer address
- Third-party payer policy number(s)
- Subscriber's name
- Subscriber's employer (if subscriber is different from patient)
- Employer phone number
- Copy of third-party coverage card
- Copy of driver's license or photo I.D.

Once collected, demographic information is accessed by the medical biller electronically or in hard copy and entered into the provider's billing system. The demographic information is used to determine who will receive a bill for the services: patient or patient representative (first-party payer) or third-party payer and patient or patient representative.

Even when a third-party payer is billed, the patient/responsible party is furnished with a copy of the bill both as a receipt for services and in the event the third-party payer only pays the claim partially or denies the claim.

Chargemaster/Fee Schedule

The chargemaster or fee schedule is a healthcare provider's comprehensive price list of all supplies, services, and equipment usage fees for patient care. Chargemaster is the term usually used for inpatient care, while fee schedule is in reference to outpatient and physician care. It may be as small as a few dozen items or may be hundreds of pages with thousands of entries, depending on the nature of the services offered by the healthcare provider.

> **Highlights**
>
> *Chargemaster* or *fee schedule* are just two of the many terms used to refer to this information. Master lists of fees may be contained in electronic healthcare management software or in hard copy.

All fee schedules generally contain these three items:

- Procedure code
- Description
- Fee

Codes are uniform from provider to provider since they must match the procedure code system (ICD-9 Volume III, CPT®, and HCPCS) adopted in the United States. Code descriptions may have some slight variation in language, but generally they are very similar since they must support the code.

The fees, however, vary from provider to provider. One provider may charge $130 for a routine office visit; another provider may charge $110.

The chargemaster or fee schedule is updated annually (at a minimum) and is available for review by auditors, third-party payers, and patients. Just to refresh your memory, here is another sample.

> We've placed a visual aid in the appendix on page 158.

I. MULTIPLE CHOICE.
Choose the best answer.

1. All chargemasters or fee schedules contain which item(s)?
   - ○ procedure code
   - ○ description
   - ○ fee
   - ● all of the above

2. The healthcare provider's comprehensive price list of all supplies, services, and equipment usage fees is referred to as the chargemaster or _____.
   - ○ procedure codes
   - ○ provider schedule
   - ● fee schedule
   - ○ master list

3. The fees on the chargemaster or fee schedule _____.
   - ○ are always the same
   - ● vary from provider to provider
   - ○ are set by the procedure code system
   - ○ do not include tax

4. How often is the chargemaster or fee schedule updated?
   - ○ every day
   - ● every year (at a minimum)
   - ○ every five years (at a minimum)
   - ○ whenever the provider decides

13

Charge Sheet/Billing Master/Encounter Form

Not every patient uses every service on a provider's charge list on every visit! Of course, it would be cumbersome to print a chargemaster every time a patient was seen just to track the charges for that visit.

Inpatient providers compile a patient charge list during an inpatient stay. Each service, supply, or procedure the patient receives is "submitted" by the department providing the service. By the end of the hospital stay, the patient's charge list detailing each service is complete and ready for use in preparing the patient's billing statement/insurance claim.

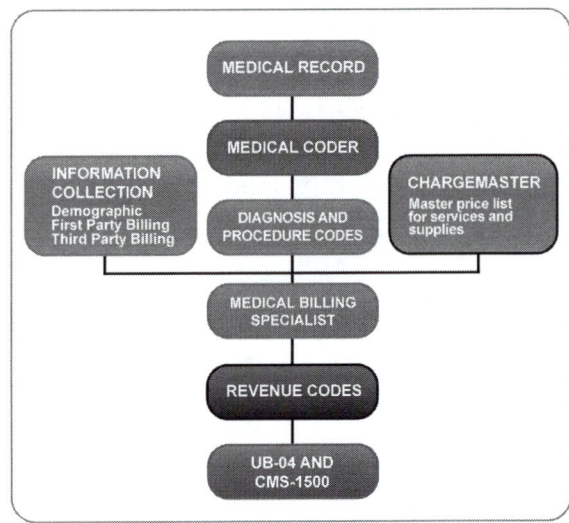

Different providers have different names for the tracking of individual patient charges. Many physician offices call them billing master, encounter forms, or charge sheets. Outpatient facilities may simply call them charges. Whatever they are called, let's track the "charge" process in two different outpatient settings: physician office and outpatient surgery clinic.

> We've placed a visual aid in the appendix on page 159.

Charge Sheets

When a patient completes an outpatient visit to a physician, the physician uses the charge sheet to record the diagnoses and the procedures performed. The charge sheet in a physician's office or small clinic usually reflects the most commonly diagnosed conditions and common procedures and supplies. The charge sheet accompanies the patient from the patient care area to the check-out area.

In this example, the patient was seen for hoarseness and sinus pressure and congestion. The physician diagnosed chronic sinusitis and hoarseness and performed a flexible laryngoscopy.

The patient takes the charge sheet to the front desk for checkout. The front office staff checks the chargemaster and, based on services, calculates the cost of the visit to be $235. The front office staff then checks the patient demographic information and, noting the patient has third-party coverage, collects a partial payment from the patient of $47 and informs the patient the third-party coverage will be billed.

The charge sheet provides the first summary of diagnosis, procedure, and supply information. Charge sheets for physician offices and other limited-service outpatient providers usually list the most common diagnoses and procedures. In many cases, the charge sheet will have a space for the physician or other provider to hand-write additional items.

Example Charge List

For our next example, let's look at an outpatient surgery center. The lists of supplies, procedures, and equipment used in an outpatient surgery center are much longer and more complex than in a physician's office. In these settings, the charge list is compiled during and after the patient's care by healthcare providers and support staff.

A surgeon's office calls the outpatient center to schedule the surgery and gives the office staff a diagnosis of chronic tonsillitis and a tonsillectomy procedure is needed. The charge list for the patient is begun when the office staff selects the diagnosis and procedure for the patient from the chargemaster list.

Diagnosis: Chronic tonsillitis
Procedure: Tonsillectomy

When the patient presents for the surgery, the medical record creation begins and, at the same time, the healthcare staff enters items on the patient's charge list, as they are ordered/used during surgery.

Patient Name: Marcia Brady
Patient Age: 12-years-old

Medical record documented IV hydration.

Charge: IV hydration 1 HR 90760
Each add'l HR 90761

> **Highlights**
>
> *Charge list, charge sheet, encounter form,* and *billing master* are different names for the form used to summarize the supplies, procedures, and diagnoses for a particular patient.

After discharge from the outpatient surgery center, all of the details are summarized on a charge sheet.

Patient Name: Marcia Brady
Patient Age: 12-years-old
Diagnosis: Chronic tonsillitis
ICD-9 Code: 474.00
Procedure: Tonsillectomy
ICD-9 Procedure Code: 28.2
CPT® Code: 42826
IV hydration 1 HR 90760
IV hydration add'l HR 90761

The charge list is a compilation of diagnoses, procedures, and supplies.

Medical Record, Medical Coder, and Codes

The charge sheet is not a substitute for a medical coder. Remember, the medical codes, descriptions, and charges must accurately reflect the information in the patient's medical record. On discharge from a healthcare visit, the patient's medical record is often still a work in progress—waiting for dictation and transcription of documents, lab results, or signatures.

Let's reconsider the example we used for the outpatient surgery center. The charge list shows the procedure as a tonsillectomy based on the scheduling of the surgery. Suppose the surgeon found the adenoids to be scarred and removed them during the surgery. The surgeon dictates the operative report with tonsillectomy and adenoidectomy as the procedure.

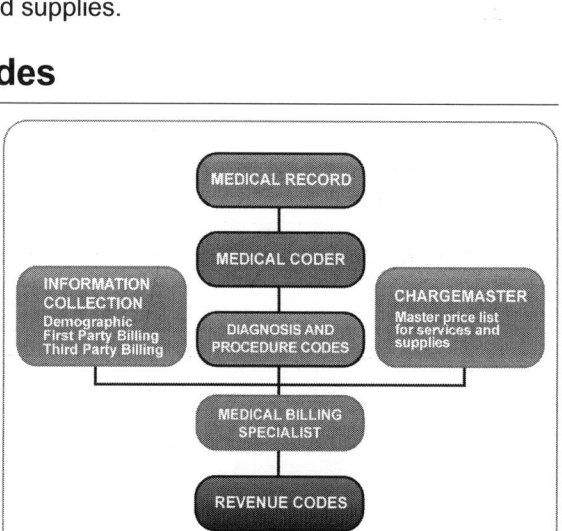

A chargemaster or encounter form is like a rough draft. The medical coder codes the diagnoses, procedures, and supplies from the medical record and passes the information to the medical biller. When the information does not match the charge list, the charge sheet is updated to reflect the correct information based on the medical record. The medical coder works with the medical biller, the medical record, and the chargemaster to go from rough draft to final form.

> **Highlights**
>
> Auditors compare medical records, codes, and bills for consistency. Charging for services not documented in the patient record is a fraudulent practice.

The demographic information, third-party billing information, charge list reflecting final diagnosis codes, procedure codes, and supply codes are the basic elements necessary for creating the UB-04 or CMS-1500 and the patient's statement.

Revenue Codes

Once the medical biller has the four necessary components (*1. demographics*, including payer information, 2. *fee* for each service from the chargemaster, 3. *charge list* with description, and 4. *correct diagnosis, procedure, and supply codes*), the medical biller is ready to add the revenue codes and create the UB-04 or CMS-1500 and patient statement.

The medical biller assigns revenue codes, often helped by an automated/integrated medical billing program. Only the UB-04 requires revenue codes. Revenue codes are 4-digit codes; they indicate inpatient or outpatient, the department (cost center) where the service(s) originated, and each 4-digit code represents a range of services. Services described by revenue codes include room (accommodation) or an ancillary service. (The leading zeros are often dropped on revenue codes, making them appear as 3-digit codes).

For example, a patient who is seen in the emergency room would have a 4-digit emergency room revenue code, a newborn in the newborn nursery would have a nursery accommodation revenue code assigned. If the patient had an x-ray performed in the emergency room, a 4-digit revenue code would be assigned for the radiology department. If the patient had lab work done, there would be a laboratory revenue code.

The medical biller assigns the revenue code based on the departments submitting charges to the charge list and the CPT® and HCPCS codes assigned by the medical coder for outpatient records. Revenue codes describe room charges and ancillary services for an inpatient (hospital) stay.

If you decide to pursue additional training in medical billing, you will learn a great deal more about the revenue cycle.

> We've placed a visual aid in the appendix on page 160.

Review: Outpatient Billing Process

I. **TRUE/FALSE.**
   Mark the following true or false.

   1. Revenue codes are reported on both the CMS-1500 and UB-04 claim forms.
      - ○ true
      - ● false

   2. A charge sheet can be used as a substitute for a medical coder.
      - ○ true
      - ● false

   3. The chargemaster is the physician's price list of all the supplies, services, and equipment usage fees for patient care.
      - ● true
      - ○ false

   4. Demographic information is used to determine who has responsibility for payment of medical services.
      - ● true
      - ○ false

   5. All providers refer to the form used to track individual patient charges as a charge sheet.
      - ○ true
      - ● false

UB-04, CMS-1500, Patient Statement

The last step in the medical billing process is the preparation of the patient statement and UB-04 or CMS-1500. In the last unit, you viewed sample UB-04, CMS-1500, and patient statements. At this time, let's take another look and identify these forms.

> We've placed a visual aid in the appendix on page 150.

> We've placed a visual aid in the appendix on page 161.

> We've placed a visual aid in the appendix on page 162.

Concluding Thoughts

In your study of the healthcare reimbursement process, we often referred to the medical billing specialist (biller) and the medical coding specialist (coder). In the outpatient setting, some healthcare providers work in small, specialized settings. In these environments, it is not at all unusual for the medical biller and medical coder to be the same person. In some cases, the front office staff is just one person who collects demographic information, codes, and bills. Of course, there are many outpatient settings where a medical coder does only coding and a medical biller does only billing, although they often work closely together. The inpatient medical coder and inpatient medical biller are rarely rolled into one.

Keep in mind as you progress in your training and your career how important it is to continue to learn and expand your knowledge. The most employable people with the most employment opportunities are those with the widest set of professional skills.

Another important piece of information to consider as you study the healthcare reimbursement process is that although the basic elements of the process are the same in each healthcare setting, the methods and procedures themselves may vary greatly. One provider may operate mostly in hard copy; another provider may be totally electronic. One provider may never send a bill that has not been coded by a medical coder; another office may have a medical coder who audits after billing and then sends corrected bills as necessary. The software for one office might automatically insert the medical coder's diagnosis, procedure, and supply codes directly onto the appropriate billing form; another office may be set up so that only the medical biller can add or delete information from the bill.

Regardless of the methodologies used by your employer, you will be able to learn to use them efficiently in your role of medical coder if you understand the healthcare reimbursement process and the elements of the billing process.

Unit 3
Life Cycle of a Claim

Life Cycle of a Claim – Introduction

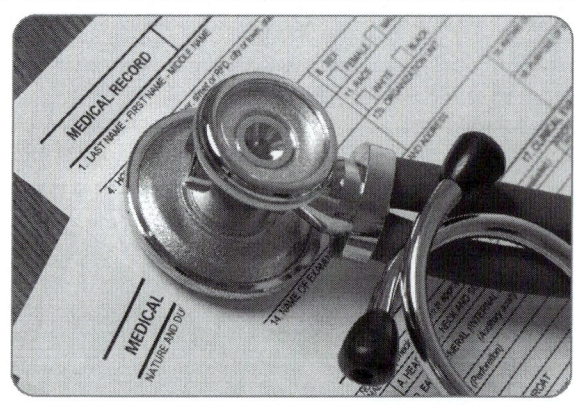

If you have ever had to deal with a disputed medical insurance claim, you probably became somewhat overwhelmed with the insurance system. When looking at a rejected medical claim, the codes and explanations—not to mention trying to speak to someone at the insurance company itself—can seem frustrating. There is, in fact, a very regimented process that insurance companies use to process the claims and since they deal with billions of claims every year, the system must be efficient.

In this unit, we will look at the process through which a typical medical claim passes. Understanding the process and how you participate and access the information when you are a coding specialist will be necessary if your position includes billing duties. You will also see that the confusing codes and explanations are really an effort to make a very large and complex system more efficient and thorough.

The Four Steps in a Medical Claim

All medical claims going through third-party payers follow the same cycle. The cycle begins when a patient with medical benefits receives medical services and a medical insurance claim is created. The cycle ends when the claim is paid. What happens in between is pretty universal, with minor exceptions depending upon the 3rd-party payer.

In its most basic form, the life cycle of a claim looks like this:

Submission   Processing   Adjudication   Payment

Submission – The sending of the claim by the healthcare provider to the 3rd-party payer. Submissions are made by mail or by a number of types of computer networks.

Processing – The third-party payer gathers information related to the case (specifics about the patient, the case, and the coverage).

Adjudication – The process of checking the details of the claim against the information the third party has on the patient and his/her insurance benefits. This process will also check for completeness of the claim, bundling issues for CPT codes, medical necessity, and recent claims (to avoid unnecessary service or duplicate claims).

Payment – A remittance advice is sent to the healthcare provider and an explanation of benefits is sent to the patient. These forms explain what was covered by the third-party payer, what was not, and why. These forms contain patient and facility information, types and dates of services, charges, type of bill, and reason and remark codes. Payment is sent to the facility for covered services.

I. **TRUE/FALSE.**
   Mark the following true or false.

   1. All medical visits produce a third-party medical claim.
      - ○ true
      - ● false

   2. Medical claims are always printed on paper.
      - ○ true
      - ● false

   3. The submission of a claim begins with the healthcare provider.
      - ● true
      - ○ false

   4. Explanations of payments or non-payments are sent to both the healthcare provider and the patient.
      - ● true
      - ○ false

   5. All third-party payers use the exact same methods of processing claims.
      - ○ true
      - ● false

Claim Submission – Documentation Preparation

Accuracy of documentation will determine how efficient the reimbursement process is. For a claim to be submitted properly, all information must be accurate, up to date, and clearly documented. Documentation is the foundation for tracking patient treatment, proving appropriateness of medical care and compliance with regulations imposed by various agencies, and provides the basis for billing healthcare services. Different outpatient providers handle the storage and integration of patient records in different ways, but as a general rule the patient's payment history is kept separate from the medical record.

21

Every outpatient visit, from a complicated trip to the emergency room to a routine followup, is tied to a specific patient and documented in a paper or electronic record (or some combination of both). You learned about healthcare documentation extensively in other modules, and once again it comes up as an important factor in healthcare reimbursement. When the patient comes in for treatment, demographic information is collected and the details of the patient's visit are recorded to form the medical record.

Information is collected from the patient regarding financial responsibility for the administered healthcare services. In many cases, this is the patient; however, a parent or legal guardian would be responsible for a minor or ward. Even when third-party payer information is provided, most healthcare providers require the patient or legal guardian to accept financial responsibility in the event the third-party payer only pays a portion of the charges or denies the claim.

> **Highlights**
>
> Each patient record has two components that may or may not be stored together:
>
> 1. The medical record component records the details of the healthcare visit.
> 2. The financial record component includes the patient's contact information, billing information, payment history, insurance cards, and financial liability form.

In physician's offices the financial responsibility form is always kept as part of the medical record.

> We've placed a multi-page visual aid in the appendix on pages 163-164.

Claim Submission – 3rd-Party Payer Information

A medical claim cannot even begin correctly if the correct insurance and billing information is not collected and kept up to date. First and third-party billing information (along with other demographic information) is usually collected by the front office when the patient comes in for treatment. Patient information is re-verified at each visit to ensure records are up to date. This information allows the submission to go to the correct place with the correct identifiers.

Front Side of Insurance Card:

I.D. Number – This identifies the patient and the patient's family members to the third-party payer.

Name – The subscriber name (employee) is typically shown here.

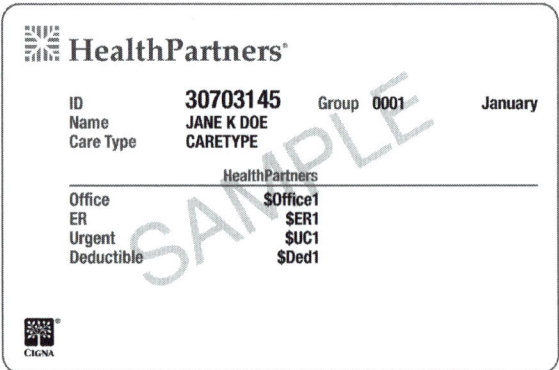

Claims Submission – Indicates where paper claims are to be mailed and how electronic claims are to be processed. There is other important information on this side of the card that pertains to verification of benefits, prior approval for services, and prescription coverage.

Care Type – Indicates the type of plan the patient has with the third-party payer.

I. TRUE/FALSE.
Mark the following true or false.

1. It is the patient's responsibility to make sure all up-to-date demographic and insurance information is on file at the healthcare provider.
    - ○ true
    - ● false

2. A financial responsibility form signed by the patient assigns the patient or guardian responsibility of any part of a claim that is unpaid by the third-party payer.
    - ● true
    - ○ false

3. In a physician's office the financial responsibility form should be kept in a separate billing file.
    - ⊘ true
    - ● false

4. It is illegal for healthcare providers to copy or duplicate patients' insurance cards.
    - ○ true
    - ● false

5. An insurance policy indicated on a single insurance card can cover more than one person.
    - ● true
    - ○ false

Claim Forms

In years past, the claims process was especially cumbersome because there was no standardization to the forms required by third-party payers. In recent years, claim forms have been standardized making the billing process more streamlined and efficient.

Outpatient providers bill third-party payers on two different claim forms: UB-04 and CMS-1500. The UB-04 is the claim form used to bill outpatient facility charges: surgery centers, freestanding radiology clinics, laboratories, and emergency rooms. The CMS-1500 is the claim form used to bill professional services: surgeon's fees for a surgery performed at an outpatient surgery center or an emergency physician's fee for professional services provided in the emergency room.

Let's look at a couple of examples:

> Dorothy cuts her finger preparing Sunday dinner and goes to the Valley Emergency Room. The ER doctor, Dr. Hanks, examines her and requests an x-ray of the finger. An x-ray is performed and read by the radiologist, Dr. Johnson. With no apparent bone or tendon involvement, Dr. Hanks stitches the laceration and discharges Dorothy.

UB-04: Emergency room facility charges, suture kit, x-ray, bandages, anesthetic, and other supplies are billed on the UB-04 as outpatient charges by Valley Hospital. The hospital bills for the facility, equipment, and supplies.

CMS-1500: Emergency room physician charges, professional services for emergency care and suturing by Dr. Hanks are billed on CMS-1500. Radiologist professional charges for Dr. Johnson's reading of the x-ray are billed on CMS-1500. The professional services are billed by the professional provider who provides services at the outpatient facility.

> Henry's orthopedist, Dr. Elfrink, recommends rotator cuff surgery since all of the conservative treatments for shoulder pain and immobility have failed. Dr. Elfrink schedules Henry's surgery at the Chugach Surgery Clinic. Henry undergoes successful same-day surgery rotator cuff repair at the Chugach Surgery Clinic.

UB-04: Chugach Surgery Clinic bills the surgery and recovery room care charges, supplies, drugs, and surgical equipment because Chugach Surgery Clinic owns the facility and the equipment and supplies used to perform the surgery.

CMS-1500: Dr. Elfrink bills professional services for performance of the rotator cuff surgery. The anesthesiologist for the surgery also bills his professional services separately on CMS-1500.

UB-04 form indicates patient demographic information at the top of the form. In the middle of the form, it lists the services rendered. The UB-04 form has a description of the services as well as a 5-digit code assigned to that service or procedure.

> We've placed a visual aid in the appendix on page 165.

I. **MULTIPLE CHOICE.**
   Choose the claim form that would be used in each situation.

   1. Jim falls on his wrist while skateboarding and goes to the emergency room where he has an x-ray. What form would be used for the x-ray charges?
      - ● UB-04
      - ○ CMS-1500

   2. What form would be used for the reading of the x-ray charges?
      - ○ UB-04
      - ● CMS-1500

   3. Jim's wrist is put in a cast. Which form would be used to charge for the casting materials?
      - ● UB-04
      - ○ CMS-1500

   4. What form would be used to charge for the doctor's professional services for casting Jim's wrist?
      - ○ UB-04
      - ● CMS-1500

Submitting a Claim

Once the patient has received healthcare services and care has been documented, codes can be assigned to the patient's medical record. Coding of the medical record is done in a couple of different ways.

In outpatient facilities where routine and/or repetitive diagnoses or procedures are done, the provider will sometimes use a charge sheet that lists several diagnoses and procedures. After the patient has received care, the provider will circle the appropriate diagnosis and/or procedure description and code on the charge sheet. This allows the front office to give the patient estimated charges and, when appropriate, collect the first-party portion of the bill. The medical coder will perform audits to make sure that all billable services are appropriately coded. Audits will be covered in a future unit of the Exploring Healthcare Reimbursement module.

In order for claims to be reimbursed efficiently and accurately, the submission process must be completed in an exacting manner. There have been some excellent advances in this process in recent years that have made the entire claims process much simpler, quicker, and more accurate.

In order for patient documentation to be sufficient for the claim, the following should be produced and maintained for each patient upon each visit:

- Patient registration
- Receipted copayment from patient
- Correctly coded encounter form. Charges will be totaled for all services performed. These same codes should be verified against the patient's medical record before the claim is filed.
- Charges should be entered into patient's account
- Claim form should be completed
- Supporting documentation (as needed) should be attached to the claim. (This is needed for certain codes that require further information or to review and verify past payments.)
- A copy of the claim should be made and stored in the carrier's facility
- Claim form to be submitted to third-party payer

The manner of the claim submission will depend upon the medical provider's system—it may be electronic or it may be paper-based. Claims submitted electronically (via the Internet or a private network) have the advantage of being received quickly, making the entire processing time quicker.

Claims Processing

The way a claim is processed depends very much upon the way the submission was made. In the past claims were traditionally submitted by mail. If you end up working in an office that still uses a paper-based system, you must carefully review the CMS-1500 for errors or omissions. Approximately 1/3 of all paper-based submissions are initially rejected due to incorrect or incomplete claim forms. These rejections will result in resubmissions that will take up valuable time and delay payment. We will work through the CMS-1500 form in great detail in the next unit.

> We've placed a visual aid in the appendix on page 150.

Paper-based claims processing looks like this:

Medicare pays home health agencies (HHAs) a predetermined base payment. The payment is adjusted for the health condition and care needs of the beneficiary. The payment is also adjusted for the geographic differences in wages for HHAs across the country. The adjustment for the health condition, or clinical characteristics, and service needs of the beneficiary is referred to as the case–mix adjustment. The home health PPS will provide HHAs with payments for each 60–day episode of care for each beneficiary. If a beneficiary is still eligible for care after the end of the first episode, a second episode can begin; there are no limits to the number of episodes a beneficiary who remains eligible for the home health benefit can receive.
(*Centers for Medicare and Medicid Services. www.cms.hhs.gov/HomeHealthPPS*)

Third-party payers receive mailed CMS forms and date them (date received).

They are organized by insurance carrier or they are scanned electronically.

Third-party payers enter the information into their own claims software.

Claim is reviewed by claims examiner for validation of information.

Recently, however, electronic submissions have become a staple of many healthcare providers. Because of new Medicare regulations, a reduced operating cost, and updated HIPAA mandates, electronic submissions are used by nearly all healthcare providers. There are several ways that electronic submissions can be made:

- *A provider may complete the claim using specialized software and submit it to the third-party payer*
- *A provider may enter essential data into a database and have a clearinghouse (see below) complete and submit the claim*
- *A provider may hire a company to complete and file the claim based on the information gathered at the office*

There are many advantages to the electronic claims submission. Using software to complete a claim form allows for an electronic review of the claim prior to submission. This eliminates many of the small errors that would otherwise create a rejection of the claim (and a delay in payment). These electronic claims can then be filed over the Internet or a similar network), cutting down on time in transit.

With the advent of the electronic claim filing came several new needs: a way to make the format of claims coming from many different types of software more universal; a need to pre-screen the electronic submissions for errors; a need to distribute the submissions to the correct third-party payers; and a need to handle data. This is where the clearinghouse comes in. A **clearinghouse** is a company contracted by the third-party payers to handle and format submissions, screen claims, and make data available to providers. The clearinghouse has pre-edits built in so claims that do not meet the clean claim requirements are sent back to

27

the providers to be reviewed, to have errors corrected, and to be resubmitted once they are correct. Only clean claims are then submitted from the clearinghouse to the third-party payer; however, this does not mean the provider will still not receive rejections on the claims that were sent on by the clearinghouse.

The clearinghouses actually save the insurance companies money because they reduce the amount of time spent reviewing claims, altering formats, and sending and receiving information to and from the providers. The electronic files are easily stored and recalled when needed. And, as with all parties involved in medical information transference, clearinghouses must meet HIPAA guidelines.

So in the end, whether filing via mail or electronically, the processing steps get the claim to right person/people in the right format so payment decisions can be made quickly and accurately.

I. MULTIPLE CHOICE.
Choose the best answer.

1. Most claims today are filed _____.
    - ○ late
    - ○ on paper
    - ● electronically
    - ○ by the coder

2. The claim itself must be filed on the _____.
    - ● CMS-1500
    - ○ AHIMA-100
    - ○ CMV
    - ○ PPO-E

3. An advantage of the electronic claim is _____.
    - ○ increased speed
    - ○ decreased errors
    - ○ decreased cost
    - ● all of the above

4. A clearinghouse acts as a liaison between _____.
    - ○ the coder and the biller
    - ○ the patient and the healthcare provider
    - ● the healthcare provider and the third-party payer
    - ○ the insurance company and the third-party payer

5. One of the duties of the clearinghouse is to _____.
    - ○ contact the patient about errors in the claim
    - ● pre-edit claims for errors
    - ○ bill patients for unpaid claims
    - ○ provide superbills to providers

Claims Adjudication

The detailed work by the payer begins in the **claims adjudication** process. By definition, *adjudication* means rendering a decision or making a judgment. While this may sound like claims are judged subjectively, the process is very objective and follows a very strict protocol.

In general, the adjudication process is as follows:

Step 1 – The adjudication process begins by comparing the patient information and demographics on the claim to the information and demographics on the policy. This verifies that the correct person is identified on the claim and that person is eligible for benefits. If the identifying information is not the same, the claim is rejected.

Medical claims are not judged or evaluated subjectively with decisions made on a whim. There are very strict guidelines payers follow when determining payment of a claim. This does not mean, however, that a payer and a physician may not have different opinions on how a claim is or is not paid.

Step 2 – The next step in the process is a check of the diagnostic and procedure codes. The codes listed on the claim are compared against those on the list of covered codes for that particular policy. The procedure codes are checked to make sure they correspond to the diagnosis codes and represent a necessary medical procedure.
At this point in the process, the claim is also checked to ensure proper authorization (or preauthorization) was obtained for any procedure that the policy states requires such. The claim may be rejected if there are codes on the claim that are not covered by the policy, if a procedure is deemed medically unnecessary, or if proper authorization was not obtained.

Step 3 – The adjudication process continues with a check of the **common data file**. The common data file is an overview of claims recently filed on the patient. It is reviewed to make sure there are no duplicate claims and to check to see if the claim is related to other procedures performed recently.

Step 4 – Next, the payer determines what the allowed charges are for each service on the claim. The **allowed charge** is simply the amount the policy states is payable for a particular procedure. Using this payment figure, the payer can then determine the **deductible** (the amount the insured must pay yearly before benefits begin) and the **coinsurance** (the percentage of the bill the patient pays once the deductible is met).

Step 5 – The adjudication process is now complete. All payment determinations have been made regarding third-party payer obligations and policyholder obligations. The next step is to inform the medical service provider and the policyholder of the determinations made.

I. **MATCHING.**
   Match the correct term to the definition.

   1. __C__ adjudication
   2. __a__ coinsurance
   3. __b__ clearinghouse
   4. __e__ common data file
   5. __d__ submission

   A. a percentage of medical bills the policyholder is responsible for after deductible is met
   B. a company that handles, formats, screens, and distributes claims
   C. the process of reviewing a claim and deciding what claims are to be paid
   D. the sending of the claim by the healthcare provider to the third-party payer
   E. an overview of claims recently filed on a patient

Claim Information

Hard Copy Notices

It is important that the there is a free flow of information between the policyholder, the healthcare provider, and the third-party payer. Because there are so many millions of claims made each year, it is impossible for payers to spend an exorbitant amount of time explaining each claim. Payers have a system of explaining the claim payment to the healthcare provider (so they will know what payments to expect and they will know how to bill the policyholder) and to the policyholder (so he/she will know what was covered and what will need to be paid).

Upon completion of the adjudication process, the third-party payer will send out a **remittance advice** (RA) or an **explanation of benefits** (EOB) to the healthcare provider. This document lists the patient and claim information and gives an explanation of the benefits covered and payments to be made. The provider will review the document for consistency and check it against the claim they filed. These are often sent electronically to expedite the process. Explanations of benefits don't all look identical although they generally contain the same types of information. The look and the details of the explanation of benefits vary from third-party payer to third-party payer. When a check or other form of payment accompanies the explanation of benefits, it is often referred to as the remittance advice. Government third-party payers' notifications to providers are also often called remittance advices.

> We've placed a visual aid in the appendix on page 166.
>
> We've placed a visual aid in the appendix on page 167.

The third-party payer will also send out an EOB to the policyholder. This contains information about the patient, the services, and the claim so the patient can review it for accuracy and completeness.

Let's look at some examples of EOBs and how they are used to explain benefits and payments:

> Alice, the patient, is the 6-year-old daughter of an employee at the local grocery store. The grocery store's insurance company, Acme Insurance, receives a claim for Alice's visit to her family physician. Because this is Alice's first claim, Acme Insurance contacts the grocery store to make sure that Alice has been added as a dependent to the employee's policy prior to processing the claim. If the employer verifies Alice has been added as a dependent, the insurance company will continue processing the claim. **If the grocery store does not show Alice has been added to her parent's policy, the claim will not be processed.**

In the instance where Acme insurance checked with the grocery store and found Alice was not added to the employee's policy, an explanation of benefits would be sent to the family physician showing Acme's determination that no payment is made because Alice is not covered by the policy.

> Hartford Medical has received a claim for a routine office visit for Emily. Hartford has determined that Emily is covered and the claim is medically appropriate. The reviewer looks up the details of Emily's policy. The policy states Emily must pay the first $200 in medical expenses each calendar year, and then the charges are paid 80% by the insurance company and 20% by the patient. The reviewer determines Emily has already paid $200 this year, so the insurance company pays 80% of the allowed amount to the doctor's office. Emily receives a statement from her insurance coverage showing their benefit determination and a bill from her physician for the remaining 20%.

An explanation of benefits would be sent to Emily's physician's office and to Emily. The explanation of benefits would show the date of visit, the provider, the total charge, the amount covered by the insurance, and the amount Emily is responsible to pay based on Hartford's 80/20 determination of benefits.

Inquiries

A patient or provider need not wait until the EOB is received to find out what is happening with a claim. The status of a claim can be accessed any time during or after the claim process by making an **inquiry**. An inquiry can be made via a written request, but technology has made inquiries quicker and more up-to-date. Most healthcare providers will have electronic access to a claim's status, allowing them to see where in the process that particular claim is.

Providers may make inquiries via mail, computer, or phone for several reasons. Perhaps the payer has not responded to a claim in a timely manner (it usually takes 4 to 6 weeks for paper-based submissions, less for electronic submissions). Or maybe the claim was completed but payment was not made. Maybe there was a discrepancy in the amount paid and the amount indicated on the completed claim. It could be that there is a difference in the codes that were submitted and the codes that were listed on the Remittance advice. This happens when an insurance company's coverage policies exclude coverage for an appropriately submitted procedure code. The remittance advice sent by the insurance company may list the code for the procedure that they will cover in lieu of the originally submitted code. It is important to remember to submit the appropriate code for the actual procedure performed and not the code that the provider knows the insurance company will cover. Coding based on insurance company coverage policies is inappropriate reporting and may be viewed as fraud.

Managing Claims

As a medical coder/biller, you will be obligated legally and professionally to maintain medical claims in an organized, easily accessible system. According to the CMS, any claims filed to Medicare, Medicaid, or any other government entity must be kept for at least 5 years. If the claim was made electronically, the superbill or encounter form used to create the claim and the remittance advice must be kept for the same amount of time.

Claims will be kept in two files: open claims and closed claims.

> **Open/Pending claims** – claims that have not yet completed the claims processing cycle. Open claims may have been recently submitted, re-submitted, or appealed; whatever the case, they have not been completed.
>
> **Closed/Paid claims** – claims for which the entire process has been completed. Open and closed claims may be organized and filed by date and/or the third-party payer to whom they were submitted.

A billing clerk or billing specialist in the provider's office will be responsible for keeping track of paid and unpaid claims and remainders. There are a couple of ways that this can be done. Most offices will run an **aging report** that reconciles claims by date (current, 30 days unpaid, 60 days unpaid, etc.). The biller can then look into the unpaid claims and take appropriate action. Some offices may use a **claims log** or **claims register** into which all claims are entered. They are first put into the log when the claims are filed and all applicable information is included in the log. When payments are received, they are reviewed for accuracy and entered into the log. Any notes needed regarding the payment, patient billing, or status of the claim may be entered.

> We've placed a visual aid in the appendix on page 168.
>
> We've placed a visual aid in the appendix on page 168.

The medical biller will reconcile the closed claims and bill the first-party payer (policyholder) for any remaining charges. Statements that show date of service, service provider, and itemized charges are standard for billing first-party payers.

> We've placed a visual aid in the appendix on page 169.

As a medical biller, you may have extensive financial duties at the end of each month. If you are in charge of finances for the office, you will be expected to post all charges and deposits and make sure that all aging reports are up to date and all invoices have been sent. The exact way in which this is done will depend upon the type of office in which you work, your individual duties in regard to billing, your employer's preferences, and the billing software/system used.

Of course, one of the most time-consuming parts of medical billing will be following up on claims that have been denied, rejected, or paid at a reduced rate. The physician and his/her staff may question the validity of the rejection or reduced payment and decide to follow up on the claim. In this case, before filing an appeal, a polite phone call should be made to see if the issue can be resolved. If it cannot, a letter should be sent to the payer stating that, in the physician's judgment, there has been an incorrect payment of the claim.

I. MULTIPLE CHOICE.
Choose the best answer.

1. Who typically needs to review EOBs and RAs sent by the third-party payers?
   - ○ the policyholder
   - ○ the healthcare provider
   - ● both A and B
   - ○ neither A nor B

2. To maintain an accurate record of claims and payments, many healthcare providers will use what?
   - ○ a common data file
   - ● an aging report
   - ○ coinsurance
   - ○ secondary insurance

3. In a physician's office who is ultimately the person in charge of deciding whether or not to follow up on a denied claim?
   - ○ the coder
   - ○ the biller
   - ○ the patient
   - ● the physician

4. How can inquiries pertaining to a claim can be made?
   - ○ by mail
   - ○ electronically
   - ○ by phone
   - ● all of the above

5. Which of the following is NOT a reason to make an inquiry about a claim?
   - ○ A payment is made but not for the correct amount.
   - ○ A claim is not processed on time.
   - ● A remittance advice is sent to the healthcare provider.
   - ○ The codes on the RA do not match those on the claim.

Appealing Claims

The fact of the matter is that claims are not always paid. Throughout this unit, we have mentioned many reasons why a claim may not be paid. When a claim is denied, you will gather all of the information relevant to the claim and review it: the claim form, the remittance advice, the remark codes by each claim line explaining why this claim was rejected, the patient's medical record, and the 3rd-party payer's fee schedule (if one is provided). If a review of these forms seems to support a payment of the claim—and if that support is well documented—the physician may wish to appeal the claim.

> **Appeals are often made if:**
>
> A claim is denied for lack of pre-authorization but there were evident reasons why pre-authorization could not be obtained.
>
> A claim is denied because the payer deems a procedure not medically necessary, yet the physician believes it was medically necessary.
>
> The third-party payer denies a claim based on a preexisting condition that the physician does not believe falls under the terms of preexisting conditions.
>
> Payment is denied without reason or a lower payment is made without adequate explanation.
>
> Services are bundled and only the one of the bundled codes will be reimbursed.
>
> No modifiers are used (however, the third-party payer will not directly tell you this is missing).

The appeal process may vary slightly depending upon the third-party payer, but most of the steps are very similar. The appeal must be made in writing and must state the reason for the appeal (some carriers, like Medicare and Tricare, have forms to be filled out that will act as the written request). Since most carriers have a set time in which an appeal must be made, timeliness is important. Make sure you are aware of the window in which appeals must be started and date and make copies of all documents used in appeals process. Attached to this written appeal will be all supporting documents and records.

Following Up on Appeals

The third-party payer will review the appeal. (They usually have internal time limits on their review process, as well—typically 30 days.) They will inform the provider of their decision through a phone call or a letter. If you are unsatisfied with the decision, the carrier may allow for one or more followup "levels" of appeal. At this point, if the payer's decision is still unsatisfactory, there are steps that can be taken. Some carriers will use an objective peer review. The **peer review** is a group of physicians who can look at the claim and the supporting documentation and arbitrate the differences between the payer and the provider. They can decide, based on the medical care, the necessity of the procedures, and the payments made, whether the healthcare provider is entitled to a payment.

Government insurers, such as Medicare and Tricare, have more prescribed steps in the appeal and review process. These should be followed exactly and within the time limits set forth by their guidelines. For more information on Medicare appeals, visit their website: http://www.medicare.gov/Basics/appealsoverview.asp.

For Tricare appeals information, visit their website: http://www.tricare.mil/FACTSHEETS/viewfactsheet.cfm?id=305.

I. **TRUE/FALSE.**
   Mark the following true or false.

   1. Documentation is important to making an appeal.
      - ● true
      - ○ false

   2. If a physician believes a treatment was medically necessary but the insurance company does not, the provider can appeal the claim.
      - ● true
      - ○ false

   3. Once an appeal is denied, the appeals process has ended.
      - ○ true
      - ● false

   4. Peer reviews are done by adjudicators from insurance companies.
      - ○ true
      - ● false

   5. Appeals processes vary from one third-party payer to the next.
      - ● true
      - ○ false

Unit 4
Completing the CMS-1500 Claim Form

Completing the CMS-1500 Claim Form – Introduction

In the second half of the twentieth century the healthcare industry recognized a need to organize and centralize the medical claims process. At the time, there were several different types of claim forms being used for the many available private and government carriers. The American Medical Association teamed up with the Centers for Medicare & Medicaid Services (CMS) and the result was a uniform claim document that nearly all providers and payers could use—the CMS-1500 Claim Form.

While a government committee continues to standardize and adapt the form to be efficient and safe in the electronic age, the 1500 that we now use is not very different from the original form.

You have seen this throughout the program, but take another look at the CMS-1500. Get to know it. By the end of this unit, you are going to be best friends with this form!

> We've placed a visual aid in the appendix on page 150.

Because this form is so important to the medical claim reimbursement system, we are going to walk through the process of completing the form for a claim. The standards for the 1500 Claim Form are very exacting, and not being precise and consistent in filling out the form can lead to a claim's rejection. Each rejection and its consequential resubmission uses valuable time for the billing/coding professional (which equates to money) and a delay in the payment of the claim.

Today, nearly all claims submissions are electronic. There are very few healthcare providers that are eligible to submit by hand (they can petition to submit by hand if hardware/software requirements impose an insurmountable financial burden). While you will most likely always use electronic submissions in your work as a coder/biller, it is imperative that you understand the CMS-1500 Claim Form in its entirety. When questions, problems, or rejections arise, you need to understand what part of the form is in question and what the requirements for that part of the form are. So to that end, we are going to go through the form as if you were filling it out by hand. We will, however, include comments and tips for filling out the form for different payers (mainly Medicare) and when using software.

Preparing Documentation

We have said all along that accurate and complete documentation of patients and encounters is vital. When filling out the CMS-1500, all of the information you have gathered will be used and verified by the clearinghouse and carrier, so this information must be current and complete.

In order to fill out the CMS-1500 Claim Form, you will need several pieces of documentation at hand:

The patient registration form – This contains the patient's demographic information and insurance carrier information. This information must be up to date, and most practices will institute a policy of verifying the information upon each visit. This form is usually accompanied by photocopies of the insurance card(s) to ensure accurate spelling, group numbers, and contact information.

The patient health record – The health record is comprised of all of the information pertaining to the assessment and treatment of the patient. Generally, these will be separated by encounter.

The superbill/encounter form – This preprinted form is filled out on each visit and contains the codes that are used in the particular healthcare setting. This form will have the diagnosis codes and procedure codes marked on it by the physician at the completion of the encounter.

> We've placed a visual aid in the appendix on page 159.

You will also need several of your professional tools to check the accuracy of information and codes from the visit. Accuracy is paramount! You will need:

ICD-9 codebook

CPT codebook

HCPCS codebook

I. TRUE/FALSE.
Mark the following true or false.

1. The CMS-1500 was created to unify a scattered system of healthcare reimbursement claim styles.
   - (•) true
   - ( ) false

2. Most coders/billers will fill out their claim forms by hand.
   - ( ) true
   - (•) false

3. The encounter form/superbill is vital because it contains all of the patient's demographic information.
   - ( ) true
   - (•) false

4. You will use your codebooks to verify the codes that appear on the documentation from the patient's visit.
   - (•) true
   - ( ) false

5. Demographic information for a patient can change from one visit to the next.
   - (•) true
   - ( ) false

The Paper Claim

A claim can be made in one of two ways: on paper or in electronic format. We are going to begin with the paper claim. Even though much of the healthcare industry's information transfer has become electronic, there are still CMS-1500 paper claims made for small physician offices. Again, understanding the process is crucial to efficient and accurate claims submissions.

When we use the term **paper claim**, we are referring to any form that is submitted to the third-party payer on paper, whether it is typed or completed on a computer and printed on the computer's printer.

CMS-1500 forms completed in paper form are usually done using computer software that allows the biller to enter the information into the program and print it out on the CMS-1500 form. Some billers/coders still use a typewriter and type the information onto the form. Because many third-party payers will use an optical scanner to convert a paper claim to an electronic format, the paper claim must be filled out following some very strict guidelines (otherwise, the scanner cannot read it). You will notice the CMS-1500 Claim Form has three boxes in both the upper-left and upper-right margins with the word *PICA* beside them. This is there so the biller can check the alignment and type size of the typewriter or printer. A pica is a measurement of text that is used in design and print. In a hand submission, a size 10 print will fit into those boxes correctly. Misalignment resulting in an error in scanning is a viable reason for claim rejection. In an electronic submission, those boxes are not used.

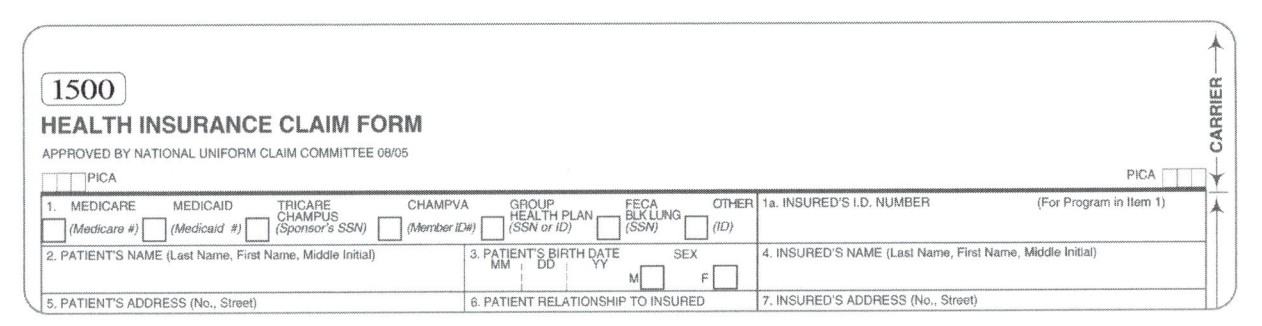

> **Highlights**
>
> Today, nearly all CMS-1500 forms are filed electronically as mandated by the Administrative Simplification Compliance Act. Some practices may apply for a waiver and be granted permission to use the paper form for submissions if:
>
> 1. They have fewer than 10 full-time employees
> 2. The submissions are for vaccinations given in a place where use of a computer would not be hygenic or possible (senior center)
> 3. The submissions are to Medicare and have more than one primary payer

Beginning Your CMS-1500: Items 1-3

When you look at the CMS-1500, you see that the form is broken into sections by dark dividing lines and each section is broken into smaller **fields**, or boxes. The sections are labeled on the right side and arrows are used to show the demarcation of the individual sections.

Carrier Information

The first section is marked "CARRIER" just to the right of the right-hand PICA boxes. Although there are no individual smaller fields in this large blank area, this is where the name and address of the third-party payer handling the claim will go. This will be typed in its entirety *in all capital letters with no periods or commas*. The only punctuation you may have in the carrier block is a hyphen in a zip code that has a 4-digit suffix. For most of you, this will look strange because it is not what we are used to seeing in proper addresses, but it is necessary for your claim to be clean. Throughout the CMS-1500, all letters will be capitalized and limited punctuation will be used (we will address the punctuation exceptions individually).

1500								CHAMPION INSURANCE CLAIMS DEPARTMENT 1463 ELM DRIVE LINCOLN TN 12345	
HEALTH INSURANCE CLAIM FORM									
APPROVED BY NATIONAL UNIFORM CLAIM COMMITTEE 08/05									
☐ PICA									PICA ☐
1. MEDICARE ☐ (Medicare #)	MEDICAID ☐ (Medicaid #)	TRICARE CHAMPUS ☐ (Sponsor's SSN)	CHAMPVA ☐ (Member ID#)	GROUP HEALTH PLAN ☒ (SSN or ID)	FECA BLK LUNG ☐ (SSN)	OTHER ☐ (ID)	1a. INSURED'S I.D. NUMBER YTH8568477882		(For Program in Item 1)
2. PATIENT'S NAME (Last Name, First Name, Middle Initial) JOHNSON MELANIE J				3. PATIENT'S BIRTH DATE MM DD YY 04 18 1972	SEX M ☐ F ☐		4. INSURED'S NAME (Last Name, First Name, Middle Initial) JOHNSON MELANIE J		
5. PATIENT'S ADDRESS (No., Street)				6. PATIENT RELATIONSHIP TO INSURED			7. INSURED'S ADDRESS (No., Street)		

The next section of the Claim Form is marked "PATIENT AND INSURED INFORMATION."

Item 1 will require you to identify the insurance type held by the patient. The correct insurance type will be marked with a capital X

Item 1a is the identifying number of the person who is insured by the policy. This is found on the insurance identification card. (Remember when we gathered all of our documentation together?)

Item 2 will include the patient's full name—last name, first name, middle initial. Do not use punctuation or suffixes (e.g. Jr., III) unless it appears that way on the patient's insurance card.

Item 3 contains two fields. The first piece of information in this field is the patient's date of birth. This must be entered in the MM DD YYYY format (e.g. 09 22 19XX). There is also a place to indicate whether the patient is male or female in this field.

I. MULTIPLE CHOICE.
Choose the best answer.

1. Which of the following is a correct entry line in the CARRIER section?
   - ○ 220 N. LAKE DR.
   - ○ 220 North Lake Drive
   - ● 220 NORTH LAKE DRIVE
   - ○ 220 North Lake Drive

2. When "checking" a box in a field, what mark should you use?
   - ○ Ã
   - ○ x
   - ○ *
   - ● X

3. Which of the following would be a correct entry for Item 2?
   - ○ Jack Smith Jr.
   - ○ Jonathon A Smith
   - ● SMITH JONATHON A
   - ○ SMITH, JONATHON A

4. All patients will need to provide what information?
   ○ insurance carrier
   ○ insurance identification number
   ○ type of insurance held
   ● all of the above

5. Which of the following would be a correct entry for Item 3?
   ● 08 10 1996
   ○ 8 10 1996
   ○ 08-10-1996
   ○ 08 10-'96

Patient and Insured information: Items 4-9

Item 4 requires the insured's name. This is the name of the insurance policyholder (which may be the same as the patient). The name should be entered last name, first name, middle initial. Do not use suffixes (e.g. Jr., III) unless it appears that way on the patient's insurance card.

Item 5 will contain the patient's full address. It is broken into spaces for the street address, city, state, zip and telephone number. Enter these without any punctuation. The exception will be if the zip code contains a 4 digit suffix, it will be separated from the first five digits by a hyphen. Use no spaces or hyphens in the telephone number (the parentheses for the area code are provided).

Item 6 indicates what the relationship the patient is to the policyholder. If the patient is the policyholder, then self would be marked with an X.

Item 7 requires the full address of the insured to be entered. This should follow the same format as item 5.

Item 8 is required by some third-party payers. It asks for the marriage and employment status of the patient, and this may change from visit to visit, causing incorrect or out-of-date demographic information.

Item 9 asks for the other insured's name. This will be used if the patient is covered by secondary health coverage. The name of the policyholder of this secondary coverage will be entered in the same manner as the name in item 4.

The next few items all hinge upon whether there is a secondary insurer entered into Item 9:

Item 9a will include the group number of the secondary insurance. This will be written with no space and no punctuation.

Item 9b will include the birthdate (mm dd yyyy) and sex of the policyholder of the other insurance.

Item 9c asks for the employer or school attended by the policyholder of the secondary insurance.

Item 9d requires the name of the company or plan that was referenced in item 9.

1. MEDICARE	MEDICAID	TRICARE CHAMPUS	CHAMPVA	GROUP HEALTH PLAN	FECA BLK LUNG	OTHER	1a. INSURED'S I.D. NUMBER (For Program in Item 1)
☐ (Medicare #)	☐ (Medicaid #)	☐ (Sponsor's SSN)	☐ (Member ID#)	☒ (SSN or ID)	☐ (SSN)	☐ (ID)	YTH8568477882

2. PATIENT'S NAME (Last Name, First Name, Middle Initial)	3. PATIENT'S BIRTH DATE MM DD YY / SEX	4. INSURED'S NAME (Last Name, First Name, Middle Initial)
JOHNSON MELANIE	04 18 1972 M☐ F☒	JOHNSON MELANIE

5. PATIENT'S ADDRESS (No., Street)	6. PATIENT RELATIONSHIP TO INSURED	7. INSURED'S ADDRESS (No., Street)
13 MATTELL LN	Self ☒ Spouse ☐ Child ☐ Other ☐	13 MATTELL LN

CITY	STATE	8. PATIENT STATUS	CITY	STATE
MIDDLETON	WI	Single ☐ Married ☒ Other ☐	MIDDLETON	WI

ZIP CODE	TELEPHONE (Include Area Code)		ZIP CODE	TELEPHONE (Include Area Code)
53562	(842) 7790450	Employed ☐ Full-Time Student ☐ Part-Time Student ☐	53562	(842) 7790450

9. OTHER INSURED'S NAME (Last Name, First Name, Middle Initial)	10. IS PATIENT'S CONDITION RELATED TO:	11. INSURED'S POLICY GROUP OR FECA NUMBER
JOHNSON KEN D		14980

a. OTHER INSURED'S POLICY OR GROUP NUMBER	a. EMPLOYMENT? (Current or Previous)	a. INSURED'S DATE OF BIRTH MM DD YY / SEX
568405	YES ☐ NO ☒	04 18 1972 M☐ F☒

b. OTHER INSURED'S DATE OF BIRTH MM DD YY / SEX	b. AUTO ACCIDENT? PLACE (State)	b. EMPLOYER'S NAME OR SCHOOL NAME
02 25 1978 M☒ F☐	YES ☐ NO ☒	BUNYAN UNIVERSITY

c. EMPLOYER'S NAME OR SCHOOL NAME	c. OTHER ACCIDENT?	c. INSURANCE PLAN NAME OR PROGRAM NAME
BUNYAN UNIVERSITY	YES ☐ NO ☒	CHAMPION INSURANCE

d. INSURANCE PLAN NAME OR PROGRAM NAME	10d. RESERVED FOR LOCAL USE	d. IS THERE ANOTHER HEALTH BENEFIT PLAN?
CHAMPION INSURANCE		YES ☒ NO ☐ If yes, return to and complete item 9 a-d.

READ BACK OF FORM BEFORE COMPLETING & SIGNING THIS FORM.
12. PATIENT'S OR AUTHORIZED PERSON'S SIGNATURE I authorize the release of any medical or other information necessary to process this claim. I also request payment of government benefits either to myself or to the party who accepts assignment below.

SIGNED SIGNATURE ON FILE   DATE 01 20 2009

13. INSURED'S OR AUTHORIZED PERSON'S SIGNATURE I authorize payment of medical benefits to the undersigned physician or supplier for services described below.

SIGNED SIGNATURE ON FILE

I. MATCHING.
Match the correct term to the definition.

1. **a** Person who was seen by the healthcare provider.

2. **d** Person or persons covered by an insurance policy.

3. **b** Plan responsible for paying any allowable charges not covered by the primary insurance.

4. **e** The subscriber who pays the premiums and in whose name the policy is written.

5. **c** The payer that pays expenses before any other coverage.

A. patient
B. secondary coverage
C. primary coverage
D. insured
E. policyholder

Patient and Insured information: Items 10-13

Item 10 is an important one. You must mark "yes" or "no" for each of the questions regarding the patient's condition. Automobile, work, or possible liability claims are handled differently from other visits.

Item 10d is reserved for local use. Some payers will request certain information be filled in here.

The next several items deal with the insured referenced in Item 1a and Item 4.

Medicare Note

Medicare and Medicaid Only: If questions 10a or 10b are answered "YES," then Medicare or Medicaid cannot be billed as the primary insurance.

Item 11 seems out of place to some people. It is asking for the policy number of the *primary* policy as it appears on the insured's card (the insured listed in Item 4). Do not use spaces or hyphens in this field.

   Item 11a again refers to the primary policy. It asks for the insured's birthdate (mm dd yyyy) and the insured's sex.

   Item 11b asks for the employer or school attended by the person insured by the primary insurance.

   Item 11c requires the name of the company or plan that was referenced in Item 1a.

Item 12 is very important. As with all medical documentation, the use and transmission of the CMS-1500 must meet HIPAA regulations. Because third-party payers require access to each patient's medical record, you will be required to obtain a signed release of medical information from each patient. While Item 12 has a place for patients to sign for the release of their medical records, nearly all healthcare providers today use a form specific to their facility that patients will sign giving permission to release medical information to their insurance company. If you have a signed and dated release of information on file (and it is not out of date), you will fill in "Signature on File" or "SOF." If you do not have an authorization on file, you will leave this space blank or enter "No Signature on File."

Item 13 is different from Item 12. While the information on the back of the CMS-1500 regarding Item 12 directs the reader to obtain permission to release medical records, Item 13 is asking for the reader to obtain permission to authorize payment from the third-party payer to the healthcare provider. Again, if you have a signed and dated release of information on file (and is not out of date), this should also contain an authorization of payment permission. If this is the case, you will fill in "Signature on File" or "SOF." If you do not have an authorization on file, you will leave this space blank or enter "No Signature on File."

With the completion of Item 13, the PATIENT AND INSURED INFORMATION section is complete.

You need to remember that the instructions we are presenting are not specific to any one payer. Medicare, Tricare, Medicaid and certain private payers may have slightly different requirements for the different fields in the CMS-1500. To verify or find further instruction and examples, check the National Uniform Claim

Committee's instructions found here: http://www.nucc.org/images/stories/PDF/claim_form_manual_v5-0_7-09.pdf.

I. TRUE/FALSE.
Mark the following true or false.

1. The policyholder and the patient are always the same person.
    - ○ true
    - ● false

2. Since most claim forms today are completed electronically, it is not necessary to have signed permission to release patient records.
    - ○ true
    - ● false

3. Authorization is needed by the patient to have the insurance company make payments to the healthcare provider that submitted the claim.
    - ● true
    - ○ false

4. The insured's birthdate must match the policyholder's birthdate.
    - ● true
    - ~~○ false~~

5. In Item 10, three fields must be "checked."
    - ● true
    - ○ false

43

Beginning the Patient or Supplier Information: Items 14-18

So far there are no real curve balls in the Claim Form. Lots of boxes, lots of information requests, but you are looking for a career in the healthcare information management field so that should be second nature to you.

Physician or Supplier Information

If you look once again to the right margin of the form, you will see the next section of the CMS is titled "PHYSICIAN OR SUPPLIER INFORMATION." In these boxes you will be entering information that will tell the story of when, why, what and where of the specific patient listed on this claim (the when—box 14, the why—box 21, the what—box 24-D, the where—box 24-B and box 32). Accuracy in all of these boxes is critical to properly inform the third-party payer of the details of the encounter. One wrong digit in the wrong box or numbers in a code transposed and the claim would be sent back as unprocessable due to invalid information.

Let's take a look at the individual items in the order in which they appear on the form.

> **Item 14** asks for the date of the current illness, accident, or pregnancy. Since there are really three options here as to the nature of the encounter, we need to understand what they are requesting for each. Again, dates will be given in the mm dd yyyy format.
>
>> If the claim is for an **illness**, the date of the first symptom recorded in the health record should be used. If no date is given, the date of service (Item 24) will be used.
>>
>> If the claim is for an **injury,** the date of the accident or injury will be entered. This is absolutely required for Worker's Compensation claims and automobile accident claims.
>>
>> If the claim is for a **pregnancy**, the date of the last menstrual cycle is used.
>
> **Item 15** seems a bit odd after filling out the previous item. It asks for dates of similar illnesses. This item is not often used. It would be used if the documentation clearly indicates the patient had a similar illness at a prior date that is also documented. Medicare and many private insurers do not require this information and it should be left blank.
>
> **Item 16** really deals solely with worker's compensation claims. These fields will have the beginning and ending dates the patient was unable to work (mm dd yyyy). Check with individual payers as to the requirements for this item because most do not require this to be filled in.
>
> **Item 17** requires the full name and the professional credentials of the physician who referred the service/supplies or who ordered the service/supplies. Even if a service was referred or ordered by a physician and was completed by a technician, the ordering physician's name goes in this space. The name is written first name *space* middle initial *space* last name *space* professional credentials. Do not use any punctuation.
>
>> **Item 17a** is no longer used as it was replaced by the NPI number (Item 17b).
>>
>> **Item 17b** is where the National Provider Identifier number will go. HIPAA required all physicians and anyone else who will be reimbursed by insurance companies to apply for one of these numbers. The main purpose was to ease medical information transference. These numbers can be found on the National Plan and Provider Enumeration System here.

44

Item 18 is used when a physician admits a patient to a hospital for any length of stay. The coder/biller would enter the date of admission in the "from" box and the date the patient is discharged from the hospital in the "to" box.

14. DATE OF CURRENT: ILLNESS (First symptom) OR INJURY (Accident) OR PREGNANCY(LMP) MM DD YY 02 13 2009	15. IF PATIENT HAS HAD SAME OR SIMILAR ILLNESS. GIVE FIRST DATE MM DD YY	16. DATES PATIENT UNABLE TO WORK IN CURRENT OCCUPATION FROM 02 13 2009 TO 04 19 2009
17. NAME OF REFERRING PROVIDER OR OTHER SOURCE DARLENE BROWN MD	17a. 17b. NPI 9371048686	18. HOSPITALIZATION DATES RELATED TO CURRENT SERVICES FROM 02 13 2009 TO 02 20 2009

I. MULTIPLE CHOICE.
Choose the best answer.

1. When filling out item 14 for an injury, the date entered would be _____.
   - ○ the date of the visit to the healthcare provider
   - ○ the date of the claim
   - ● the date of the injury
   - ○ the date of the first treatment

2. Item #18 deals with inpatient hospital length of stay. A patient was in the hospital on February 13, 2009–February 20, 2009. How would the dates appear in item #18?
   - ○ 021309 021309
   - ● 02132009 02202009
   - ○ 2132009 2132009
   - ○ 21309 21309

3. The dates in item 16 deal with _____.
   - ○ dates that the patient was seen
   - ○ dates the patient was injured
   - ● dates the patient could not work
   - ○ "from" and "to" dates the patient was ill

4. NPI numbers are required for _____.
   - ○ all clearinghouses
   - ● any healthcare provider seeking reimbursement
   - ○ patients injured in a work-related accident
   - ○ physicians only

5. An accurate entry for item 17 would be _____.
   - ○ Wilson, Allen A MD
   - ○ ALLEN WILSON, MD
   - ○ ALLEN A WILSON
   - ● ALLEN A WILSON MD

Patient or Supplier Information: Items 19-23

Item 19 states that it is "reserved for local use." As the description says, some third-party payers want this box left blank, while others will instruct you to put various information in here based on different circumstances. All third-party payers will want you to put information in this box if you are billing a NOC CPT code or if you are billing a NOC drug. Please refer to the individual payer for requirements for Item 19.

14. DATE OF CURRENT: ILLNESS (First symptom) OR INJURY (Accident) OR PREGNANCY(LMP) MM DD YY 02 13 2009	15. IF PATIENT HAS HAD SAME OR SIMILAR ILLNESS. GIVE FIRST DATE MM DD YY	16. DATES PATIENT UNABLE TO WORK IN CURRENT OCCUPATION FROM 02 13 2009 TO 04 19 2009	
17. NAME OF REFERRING PROVIDER OR OTHER SOURCE DARLENE BROWN MD	17a. 17b. NPI 9371048686	18. HOSPITALIZATION DATES RELATED TO CURRENT SERVICES FROM 02 13 2009 TO 02 20 2009	
19. RESERVED FOR LOCAL USE		20. OUTSIDE LAB? [X] YES [ ] NO	$ CHARGES 1353
21. DIAGNOSIS OR NATURE OF ILLNESS OR INJURY (Relate Items 1, 2, 3 or 4 to Item 24E by Line) 1. 719 46 3. 2. 715 96 4.		22. MEDICAID RESUBMISSION CODE ORIGINAL REF. NO. 23. PRIOR AUTHORIZATION NUMBER 9812375923	

As you can see this box is used for many different situations. Sometimes a little notebook to keep track of what a third-party payer requires in some of these boxes is not a bad idea, especially when you are just getting started. You will be surprised how much will be second nature after a couple of months.

Item 20 is used for Medicare only. It is used when a physician pays an outside entity to perform a service. If the physician has an agreement to pay for the service himself and he wants to be reimbursed for the service, he will mark "yes" and enter the amount he paid for it. Payment is entered with no dollar sign and no decimal point and will all be entered to the left of the vertical dividing line.

Item 21 contains spaces for ICD-9 diagnosis codes to be entered. A maximum of four codes can be entered. Depending on the medical billing software you will be working on, you may either enter the ICD-9 diagnosis codes without the period or you will place the period in the appropriate place.

> **Medicare Note**
>
> For Medicare only there are a few other times when box 19 needs information filled in:
>
> A. When a patient who sees a non-participating physician and the physician decides to participate on this claim but the patient refuses to assign benefits. Then enter in box 19 the following statement: "Patient refuses to assign benefits." In this case, the payments can only be made to the beneficiary.
>
> B. When physicians share post-operative care on a patient, then enter a 6 digit or 8 digit assumed date of care or relinquished date of care in box 19.

Item 22 would not be needed in a perfect world. Alas, that is not the case. This box pertains to Medicaid only. You only use it when you are resubmitting a rejected claim for additional money or if there was a coding error that you have corrected. The code is typically the rejection code for that particular claim line and the original reference number is a number that has been assigned by Medicaid for that particular claim line. You will want to verify with the state that you are working in what they expect when resubmitted a corrected claim.

Item 23 will be used if the third-party payer requires a preauthorization or precertification of a service. Usually these are reserved for inpatient services, but there are some outpatient services that require these. Medicare does not require preauthorization for services. Preauthorization/precertification numbers should be written with no spaces or punctuation.

Patient or Supplier Information: Item 24

Item 24 is the most detailed item concerning the encounter that there is on the CMS-1500. Item 24 is broken down into many parts allowing you to give details of exactly *what* happened and *when* it happened.

Item 24A requests the dates of service in a "from___ to ___" format. Here you report the dates of service in a mmddyyyy format (no spaces) because there are dividing lines embedded in the form. If you are reporting one day of service only, fill in the "from" column and put in the same date in the "to" column. You should not leave this column blank (or it may cause a rejection). However, if your physician saw a patient in the hospital for subsequent daily visits, you would enter in the "from" column the first date of the "subsequent visits" for that one code and in the "to" column enter the last day the physician visited for the same CPT® code.

Item 24B requires you to code the place of service (POS) for each of the corresponding service dates. The POS codes are standard for every third-party payer. Every physician's office can create an internal code for the different place of services to distinguish one hospital from another if the physician(s) goes to multiple hospitals. The following is a sample chart of the standard POS codes recognized by all third-party payers.

POS CODE	PLACE OF SERVICE NAME
11	Physician Office
12	Patient's Home
13	Assisted Living
21	Inpatient Hospital
22	Outpatient Hospital
23	Emergency Room - Hospital
31	Skilled Nursing Facility
20	Urgent Care

Item 24C is generally only used for Medicaid. Here you indicate whether or not the patient's treatment was an emergency by marking Y (yes) or N (no).

Item 24D is broken into one large box with four small boxes. These allow for complete procedure, service, or supply codes. In the first box enter the CPT or HCPCS code. The remaining four boxes are used for up to four modifiers (a two-digit modifier per box). There is a note to explain unusual circumstances (which would apply to a modifier 99—unlisted code). In this instance, you would be required to attach the patient's medical record and/or a written explanation of the service or procedure.

Item 24E asks for the diagnosis pointer. The pointer is the corresponding number from Item 21 (the diagnosis codes). This allows the payer to verify the procedure is appropriate for the diagnosis. Make sure you enter the single-digit list number in this box and **not** the diagnosis code.

Item 24F requires careful attention. Here you enter the charges in dollars and cents, which are separated by the embedded vertical line, for each procedure. Use no dollar signs or commas.

Item 24G requests the days or units for each service. Most services/procedures that are billed will have a unit of 1 since most services/procedures can only be billed once per 24 hours. However, there are always exceptions: if a medication comes in 15mg and the physician wants the patient to have 30mg, then the units would be 2 because 2 15mg units were given to the patient. Another example of billing multiple units would be billing subsequent hospital days. Remember, box 24A has "from" and "to" columns for the dates of service. The number of units counted would be the number of days starting with the date in the "from" column, all the days in between and including the date in the "to" column. The number you come up with is entered in the "units" column.

Item 24H pertains to Medicaid patients only. There is a special exam and form that needs to be filled out when performing this special exam. ESPDT- Early Screening Periodic Diagnosis and Treatment for children from birth to age 21. If the physician participates in this program, he must indicate if he has performed this evaluation on the claim form for appropriate reimbursement.

Item 24I may not be used. It is where the modifier explaining the type of identification number that will go in Item 24J belongs. If your payer requires an identification number in addition to the NPI number, that number will go in the shaded area of Item 24J and the modifier will be entered in the shaded area of Item 24I.

Item 24J will require the provider's NPI number in the unshaded blank and the additional identification number (if required) in the shaded area.

Line	Date(s) of Service From	To	B. Place of Service	C. EMG	D. CPT/HCPCS	Modifier	E. Diagnosis Pointer	F. $ Charges	G. Days or Units	H. EPSDT	I. ID. Qual.	J. Rendering Provider ID. #
1	01 19 2009	01 19 2009	11		99214	25	12	110 00	1		NPI	56446408112
2	01 19 2009	01 19 2009	11		20610	RT	2	125 00	1		NPI	56446408112
3	01 19 2009	01 19 2009	11		J7321		2	300 00	1		NPI	56446408112

19. RESERVED FOR LOCAL USE
20. OUTSIDE LAB? NO $ CHARGES 1353
21. DIAGNOSIS OR NATURE OF ILLNESS OR INJURY
   1. 719 46
   2. 715 96
22. MEDICAID RESUBMISSION CODE / ORIGINAL REF. NO.
23. PRIOR AUTHORIZATION NUMBER: 9812375923

I. **MATCHING.**
   Match the correct term to the definition.

   1. **C** A number used to correspond to the ICD-9 code listed earlier in the form.
   2. **E** Unique identifier required by providers.
   3. **B** Refers to the number of days, dosages, or number of injections administered.
   4. **A** Allows dates to be shown with a beginning and ending date.
   5. **D** Identifies where a service was administered.

   A. From _____ To _____ format
   B. units of service
   C. diagnosis pointer
   D. POS
   E. NPI number

Patient or Supplier Information: Items 25-33

We are nearly finished with the CMS-1500 form. By this point in filling out a claim form, you will have looked through your documentation and your coding books and you will know this claim inside and out! Let's finish up with the final items.

Item 25 is for the provider's SSN or EIN. Every physician practice files a business name with the IRS when they apply for a Federal Tax ID number, which is also known as the Employer Identification Number (EIN). This identifies to the third-party payer which physician or physician practice rendered the services and to whom to make the check payable. It is also a verification method for the third party payer to see if this physician or physician group has reported services to them before. Another important fact is that this number is how the revenue that the practice receives is reported to the IRS. Whether entering the EIN or the SSN, no hyphens or spaces are used in this field.

Item 26 is where the patient's account number is entered. This number is assigned by the provider and should be entered with no spaces or hyphens.

Item 27 gives the third-party payer consent to mail the payment to the physician's office. For government plans such as Medicare, Medicaid and TRICARE and those third-party payers where the physician has a "signed contract," marking "yes" in box 27 means that you as the medical biller cannot bill the patient the difference between the charge amount and the allowed amount.

Item 28 indicates the total amount billed on the claim form. This is gathered by adding lines 1-6 together in Item 24F. Do not enter dollar signs, decimals, or commas.

Item 29 asks for the amount already paid and will generally be left blank when making submission to the primary insurer. If sending the claim to the secondary insurer, you would fill in the amount of the claim paid by the primary insurer. Do not use dollar signs, decimals, or commas.

Item 30 follows up on the previous two boxes. Generally this will be blank if the claim is going to the primary insurer. If the primary insurer has paid on the claim and the remainder is going to a secondary insurer, the difference would go in this box.

Item 31 requires the physician's signature, credentials, and date. If you were actually filling this out by hand, he/she would sign here or "SOF" would be entered. Software will complete this by inserting the physician's name and the date the claim is printed in the correct spaces.

Item 32 has a large space for the name and location where the service was provided. The instructions are pretty specific. Remember, no commas, periods, dashes or other forms of punctuations. These will throw off the spacing in electronic transmission of information. Most third-party payers require the following:

Line 1: Name of facility (hospital name, physician office name, physical therapist clinic name to name a few)

Line 2: Street address of facility (PO Box is not acceptable)

Line 3: City, state postal code, zip code

Item 32a is reserved for the NPI number of the service facility which is entered here with no dashes, hyphens, or spaces.

Item 32b will be left blank.

Item 33 requires you to enter the healthcare provider clinic name that is filing the claim for payment. You must keep in mind that the name that appears in this box must match the name that owns the EIN/Federal Tax ID number in box 25. You will also enter the full address (remember no punctuation is to be used unless a hyphen is needed in a 9-digit zip code), and telephone number (no parentheses, dashes, or spaces).

Item 33a is reserved for the NPI number of the facility requesting payment which is entered here with no dashes, hyphens, or spaces.

Item 33b will be left blank.

We are now finished with the instructions for the CMS-1500. Feel like you have just filled out your tax form? Well, the CMS *is* a government form, just like your tax forms. While some of the information may seem excessive or redundant, the goal of all of the information is to make information transfer accurate, safe, and efficient.

While there is a lot of information to learn, don't worry. By the time you have filed a couple of dozen claims you will become comfortable with the process.

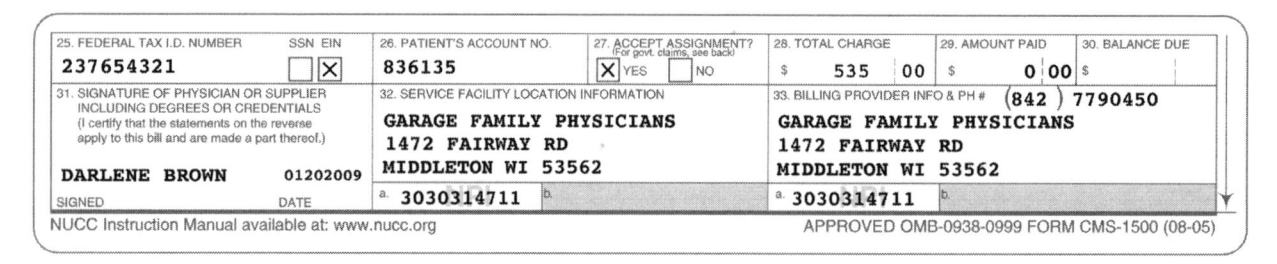

I. **TRUE/FALSE.**
   Mark the following true or false.

   1. The physician's SSN or EIN number should be entered exactly how they appear on their SSN or EIN card.
      - ○ true
      - ● false

   2. The SSN or EIN must match that filed for the clinic name in Item 33.
      - ● true
      - ○ false

   3. The physician must sign item 31 on all claims submitted.
      - ○ true
      - ● false

   4. If item 29 is left blank, that means no payment has yet been made on the claim.
      - ● true
      - ○ false

   5. Patient account numbers are universal and are assigned by insurance companies.
      - ○ true
      - ● false

Unit 5
Completing the UB-04 Claim Form

Completing the UB-04 Claim Form – Introduction

The standard documents for seeking reimbursement in the healthcare industry are the CMS-1500 claim form and the UB-04 claim form. The claim forms were created specifically for different types of medical encounters. If you remember back to the last unit, you will recall that the CMS-1500 claim form is used specifically by physicians' offices. The UB-04 form is to be used by medical facilities.

Completing the form properly is critical to ensuring reimbursements are paid in a timely manner. The UB-04, like the CMS-1500, is often completed with the aid of software specifically designed for the form. However, the software requires the proper information be gathered and entered and failing to do so can result in claim denials.

In this unit, we will look closely at the UB-04 form and how to complete it. Because the form is complex and an array of information is required, we will go through this form as if you were going to complete it by hand. We will use images of the various parts of the form to illustrate correct format and documentation.

The UB-04 Claim Form

The History of the UB-04

For many years hospitals were forced to use different claim forms for all of the different payers they were billing. Because each payer required a different form, and because each form required different information (hospital codes were not standardized), reimbursement was not guaranteed to be quick or complete. In an effort to unify and streamline the hospital billing process, the National Uniform Billing Committee (NUBC) was created in the mid-1970s. The goal of this committee was to improve the hospital billing process by creating a uniform bill that required standardized information and presented it in a standardized format.

After many drafts and trials, the first form—the UB-82—was adopted in 1982. After a period of national adoption and a continued evolution of the form, the latest revision was implemented in 2007. This version was called the Uniform Bill-04 (UB-04) and is used today for filing for reimbursement by medical facilities. The UB-04 is a red ink on white paper form, and at first glance it looks similar to the CMS-1500. Closer inspection, however, reveals a completely different document requiring a very different set of information. The UB-04 allows for compliance with all HIPAA standards and the electronic documentation transfer standards and addresses the issues of the evolving billing process, which are constantly changing in health information management.

Who uses the UB-04?

Because facilities are required to use some different codes than physicians, and because facilities provide different accommodations and supplies for patients, a different billing format is required for these facilities. The UB-04 allows for the specific charges for procedures and care supplied by facilities. Common facilities that use the UB-04 are:

- Hospitals
- Nursing homes
- Ambulatory surgery centers
- Hospices
- Rehabilitation centers

Let's look at a couple of examples of billing scenarios.

> *Alvin, an established patient, went to see his family physician with a chief complaint of a sore throat and cough. The physician performed a problem focused history and exam. The physician also performed a strep test in the office, which was positive for strep. The medical decision making was low.*

Alvin's visit would be coded for the strep throat diagnosis, the evaluation and management, and the strep test service. The encounter would then be recorded using the CMS-1500 form and submitted to his third-party payer.

> *Jake was brought to the emergency room last night by his father. His chief complaint was right upper quadrant abdominal pain, nausea, and a high fever. The emergency room physician performed a level 3 hospital emergency department visit. During the evaluation, the presence of Rovsing's sign was indicated. The physician spoke with the father, Alvin, and explained Jake needed an appendectomy and explained all risks to him. The decision to perform a laproscopic appendectomy early in the morning was made. After the appendectomy Jake was admitted to the hospital.*

Jake's visit would be coded for the diagnosis (acute appendicitis), the ER visit, an ICD-9 procedure code (which is then assigned a revenue code). The entire encounter (hospital stay) would then be assigned a DRG. The DRG information can be added once we obtain the reference book. All of the codes would be entered into the UB-04 claim form and submitted to the third-party payer from whom Jake receives coverage.

Let's take a look at the UB-04 claim form and begin going through it piece by piece.

Patient Information – Lesson 1

Let's look at the UB-04 claim form in its entirety for a moment before moving on to specific fields within the form.

> We've placed a visual aid in the appendix on page 170.

The UB-04 is a single-page form containing 81 numbered items on the front side and some additional information printed on the back of the form. The numbered items on the form are referred to as *form locators* (since they will locate items on the form). These are typically shortened to *FLs*. There are variations in the size and number of boxes within the FLs, with many of the FLs containing multiple numbered or lettered items. Another thing you will notice is that unlike the CMS-1500, the information is not grouped by the type of information requested. As we go through how to enter types of information (like patient information or healthcare provider information), we will have to jump around in the order of the form locators.

There is an electronic handbook created by the National Uniform Billing Committee called the *Official UB-04 Data Specifications Manual* that explains and defines each form locator and explains how to properly complete the form. Because many of the codes needed to complete this form will come from this manual (or from the software program you use in the medical billing department), we will refer to this manual often in this unit. It is not necessary at this time for you to have the manual, but if your career involves billing for facilities, you will probably come to know this manual very well. You can find information about this manual and the NUBC at the NUBC website.

Patient Information

We will begin by taking a look at the information on the UB-04 regarding the patient and/or the insured individual whose coverage applies to the patient. Again, most of this information will come from the demographic information received at the time of registration at the facility. The fields related to patient information begin with FL 3.

FL 3a is the first item designated for patient information. This FL asks for the patient's control number, which many facilities will call the account number. This number is assigned by the facility. Inpatient account numbers are usually tied to each encounter. Since payers are billed for each encounter, this patient control number will be unique for each visit and will be tied to the billing of that visit. This number allows payment and correspondence to be designated for each particular encounter.

FL 3b is where a permanent patient medical record number goes. This number is tied to the patient's history and information that does not change from one visit to the next. This number is also assigned by the facility.

FL 4 is titled "Type of Bill." The NUBC Data Specifications Manual has a list of the types of bills that are submitted and the corresponding codes for these types of bills (TOBs). These numbers are 4 digits in length and the first digit is always a zero. However, the zero is not used when filing the UB-04 electronically. The other digits refer to the type of facility, the classification of the bill, and the frequency of the bill.

> A common TOB number is 0131.
>
> The 0 is just a leading 0
>
> The first 1 stands for the type of facility – hospital
>
> The 3 stands for the classification of the bill – outpatient
>
> The final 1 stands for the frequency of the bill – it covers admittance through discharge

FL6 is the next patient information field. In this field you will enter the dates of admittance ("from" date) and the date of discharge ("to" date). These will be entered in the MMDDYY format. **The UB-04 requires no punctuation in most of the form locators**. Ex. From 101409 To 101709

FL 8 is titled "Patient Name" and is broken into two fields (8a and 8b). 8a is a patient identifier and is assigned by the third-party payer. If there is a patient identifier assigned that is not the same as the insurance subscriber number in FL 60, the payer may require this form locator to be filled in. Otherwise, the payer may allow it to remain blank.

FL 8b is the name of the patient and is entered in the LAST NAME   FIRST NAME   MIDDLE INITIAL format. Do not use punctuation between names.

FL 9 has spaces for FL 9a–FL9e.

> **FL9a** is the patient's mailing address. Again, all letters should be capitalized and no punctuation should be used.
>
> **FL9b** is the city.

FL9c is the two-letter state abbreviation.

FL9d is the zip code and may contain as many as 9 numbers.

FL9e is the country code and is used if the services were performed outside of the United States. Country codes can be found at this link.

Patient Information – Lesson 2

FL 10 asks for the patient's date of birth. This field is unique in that it requires a MMDDYYYY format for the date of birth (rather than a two-digit year). Ex. 12231981

FL 11 asks for patient sex and should be designated M or F.

FL 12 is used for inpatient services and home healthcare services. Here the date of the service being billed is entered in the MMDDYY format.

FL 13 is used to report the hour of admission. This is required for inpatient services, but it may not be required by the third-party payer for other types of services. The time is recorded in two-digit format using a 24-hour clock format:

Time	Hour Code
3:00-3:59 AM	03
4:00-4:59 AM	04
5:00-5:59 AM	05

The rest of the hour codes follow this same pattern.

FL 14 is used to indicate the priority of the visit based on a single-digit code assignment. These code assignments are designated by the National Uniform Bill Committee and are as follows:

Code	Priority
1	Emergency visit in which medical treatment must be immediately administered to prevent disabling, severe, or life-threatening harm.
2	Urgent visit for immediate medical treatment.
3	Planned elective services.
4	Newborns born on the same date as their admittance date, which was recorded in FL 6. This code requires a subsequent code in FL 15.
5	For trauma patients treated at a trauma center or hospital that is verified by the American College of Surgeons (ACS) or designated by state or local authority.
9	There is no information concerning priority of visit.

FL 15 requires the use of the NUBC Data Specifications Manual. This FL is where the source of the referral for the encounter is coded. Each code in the manual has a detailed description of the source of the referral. There is also a section of special codes for newborns who were born on the admittance date.

FL 16 is used to record the hour of the patient's discharge. This FL uses the same manner of recording hours that was used in FL 13.

FL 17 can be a tricky field. This is where the patient's discharge status is recorded. The status is coded by using the <u>NUBC Data Specifications Manual</u> to match a detailed description of the patient's discharge status to <u>a two-digit code</u>. These codes are often updated so using the most recent online UB-04 manual is a must.

FL 18–FL 28 There are 10 numbered boxes of equal proportion here that are for recording condition codes. The NUBC Official Data Specifications Manual lists many, many pages of condition codes that are used for indicating conditions of the claim that will ultimately give direction or information pertaining to the payment of the claim. These codes can apply to specific procedures listed on the claim form, the coverage status of a patient, details of the patient's treatment, or many of the dozens of other condition codes.

There certainly may be more than one code that applies to a claim and **all that apply must be listed**. This will take some familiarity with the different condition codes, some double checking of the NUBC Official Data Specifications Manual, and clear communication with the payers about their requirements. When listing multiple codes in these numbered boxes, they are listed from smallest number to largest number, with codes containing letters listed alphabetically after the numeric codes (e.g 01 68 AK C5).

FL 29 is used when a payer requires the state in which an automobile accident occurred be reported. Checking with the third-party payer concerning requirements will let you know if this is to be used in your billing duties.

1 Faith United Hospital	2		3a PAT. CNTL # 525252			4 TYPE OF BILL
700 LaCross Ave			b. MED. REC. # 555999			135
City XX 12345			5 FED. TAX NO.	6 STATEMENT COVERS PERIOD FROM THROUGH		7
9892223333			12-3456789	011907	012007	
8 PATIENT NAME a		9 PATIENT ADDRESS a 2014 ANNIE ST				
b STRONG WENDY		b DETROIT			c MI d 48234	e
10 BIRTHDATE	11 SEX	12 DATE ADMISSION 13 HR 14 TYPE 15 SRC	16 DHR 17 STAT	18 19 20 21 CONDITION CODES 22 23 24 25 26 27 28	29 ACDT STATE	30
07241951	F	011907 22 2 1	04 01			

I. MULTIPLE CHOICE.
Choose the best answer.

1. FL 3b differs from FL 3a because _____.
   - ○ FL 3b is always longer
   - ○ FL 3b is only for inpatient billing
   - ● FL 3b will not change from one bill to the next
   - ○ Fl 3b is only used if a patient is seen in an emergency room.

2. Code 0135 in FL 4 would indicate _____.
   - ● an outpatient encounter
   - ○ an inpatient encounter
   - ○ an emergency room encounter
   - ○ a nursing facility charge

3. A proper entry in FL 9a would be _____.
   - ○ 117 Marsh Harbour Dr.
   - ⦿ 117 MARSH HARBOUR DR.
   - ○ 117 Marsh Harbour Drive
   - ○ 117 MARSH HARBOUR DR

4. A correct entry in FL 13 for an admission that occurred at 4:20 P.M. would be _____.
   - ○ 06
   - ⦿ 16
   - ○ 04
   - ○ 14

5. Codes for FL 17 can be found _____.
   - ○ by looking at FLs 11 and 12
   - ⦿ in the NUBC Official Data Specifications Manual
   - ○ in the chart on the front of the UB-04
   - ○ by contacting the patient

Patient Information – Lesson 3

You are starting to see that the UB-04 is a complex form in which much of the information in a patient's medical record is condensed to a three-dimensional description of a patient's treatment. The challenge of a form like this is to say as much as possible without using a narrative format (which we are used to in our daily lives). We are converting the information contained in a narrative format into an alphanumeric code language that tells the third-party payers everything they need to know about the encounter.

Let's continue with the form locators dealing with patient information.

FL 30 is to be left blank at this time. It may be used in the future for recording information.

FLs 31–34 comprise four identical fields that each contain two lines for occurrence codes and two lines for occurrence dates. What is an occurrence? Anything that happens during a patient's treatment that may affect the billing/payment of the claim is an occurrence. A change in healthcare coverage during a patient's inpatient stay would require an occurrence code and the exact date of the change. The NUBC Official Data Specifications Manual lists these codes and their detailed descriptions. Again, care must be taken to make sure that these codes are as accurate and detailed as they can possibly be. The codes should be listed alphanumerically from left to right, beginning with FL31a→FL32a→FL33a→FL34a→FL31b→FL32b, etc.

FL 35 and 36 are set up just like the previous FLs except the dates have a beginning and an ending date requirement. Because of this, these are referred to as occurrence **span** codes and dates. These are for events that would affect the billing/payment of a claim for which there are a "to" and a "from" date associated with the event. These are filled out in the same order and manner as FLs 31–34 and are also listed in the NUBC Official Data Specifications Manual.

FL 37 is to be left blank at this time. It may be used in the future for recording information.

FL 38 may be required by some third-party payers. This space is used to record the name and address of the person who is responsible for the bill.

FLs 39–41 are identical boxes, each with four lettered spaces, where value codes are reported. Value codes, like occurrence codes, must be listed if they apply to the bill. Unlike occurrence codes, these codes are listed in the NUBC Official Data Specifications Manual with a monetary amount. Value codes are used to assign a dollar value to specific pieces of medical encounters. Again, this list of codes is extensive and great care must be taken in making sure the documentation matches the chosen codes. These are also listed left to right and then down the columns as needed, organizing them alphanumerically as you go.

At this point, the FLs related to the patient information skip several of the large boxes in the center of the form. (I know you were SO EXCITED to get to those giant boxes. Don't worry...we'll get to them.) Now would be a good time for a little comic relief—face it, there is not much that is humorous about government medical claim forms.

Medical Humor

At a hospital, a mother was crying at her daughter's bedside as the girl slept quietly. The mother was distraught after her daughter, while playing with her mother's pocketbook, swallowed a handful of nickels.

When the doctor came into the room, the mother stood up and asked, "Doctor, How is she."

The doctor shook his head and said, "No change yet."

Patient Information – Lesson 4

We will now skip down toward the bottom of the UB-04 and pick up the patient information with FL 50.

FL 50 is broken down into three lines—line A, B, and C. Line A is mandatory and will contain the third-party payer responsible for the claim. Many people, however, have coverage through more than one payer. The subsequent lines are available for multiple payers.

FL 51 is used to report the number that the payer uses to identify the health plan it has provided to the insured. Because FL 50 allows for multiple health plans in rows A, B, and C, a separate entry will be made for each health plan listed in item 50.

FL 52 is where the biller indicates whether the patient or the patient's guardian signed a release of information supplied by the provider. The release of information is needed so the third-party payer can use the medical information to accurately process the claim. If the provider has a signed release, this box will be filled in with a Y. Because FL 50 allows for multiple health plans in rows A, B, and C, a separate entry will be made for each health plan listed in item 50. Row A will always be entered first.

FL 53 is used to indicate whether the patient has signed a statement that assigns the benefits paid by the third-party payer to the healthcare provider. This is indicated with a Y for yes or an N for no. Like FL 52, a separate entry is required for each third-party payer listed in FL 50.

FL 54 may be required by some third-party payers. This where an amount can be entered to specify how much money has already been paid by the third-party payer.

At this point, skip down to FL 58.

FL 58 is a required field. The name of the insured person is entered here in the LAST NAME   FIRST NAME   MIDDLE INITIAL format. There will be a name listed for each third-party payer listed in FL 50.

FL 59 indicates the relationship of the patient to the insured person. There are nine possible codes that cover the possible relationships listed in the NUBC Official Data Specifications Manual. They are as follows:

Code	Relationship
01	Spouse
18	Self
19	Child
20	Employee
21	Unknown
39	Organ donor
40	Cadaver donor
53	Life partner
G8	Other relationship

Since FL 50 may have multiple entries if there are multiple third-party payers, there may be different codes for different payers, depending upon who the insured person listed in FL 58 may be.

FL 60 is used to record the subscriber's unique identification number. This number is assigned by the insurance company.

FL 61 requires the group name of the insured person if a group name is available. Again, this is entered in capital letters without punctuation.

FL 62 requires the group number if one is available.

FL 63 is used for services requiring authorization or preauthorization. When authorization is sought, a number is assigned by the third-party payer to the patient for that treatment. That number will need to match the treatment reported on the UB-04 in order for reimbursement to be paid.

FL 64 is used if a claim has already been processed and is now being sent as a voided claim or as a claim to replace the original. When a third-party payer reimburses a provider, they will provide a document control number. If you are re-sending a claim to them as a voided claim or as a replacement claim, you would need to include this number to indicate what encounter the new UB-04 is referring to.

FL 65 is used to enter the name of the employer providing coverage to the insured listed in FL 58. This form locator is not always required.

50 PAYER NAME	51 HEALTH PLAN ID	52 REL INFO	53 ASG BEN	54 PRIOR PAYMENTS	55 EST. AMOUNT DUE	56 NPI	1234512345
MEDICARE	XXX	Y	Y			57	999888
						OTHER PRV ID	

58 INSURED'S NAME	59 P.REL	60 INSURED'S UNIQUE ID	61 GROUP NAME	62 INSURANCE GROUP NO.
STRONG WENDY	18	333222555		782153

63 TREATMENT AUTHORIZATION CODES	64 DOCUMENT CONTROL NUMBER	65 EMPLOYER NAME

Form locator 65 completes the Patient Information section of the UB-04. It may have seemed endless, but at least you have the majority of the form locators behind you.

We have always emphasized the importance of documentation and now you can see how vital it is. Proper, accurate documentation would be needed for the extremely detailed information provided about the patient. You also see how all of this information has been "compressed" to a series of codes, dates, and names that a payer can decipher and use to adjudicate the claim.

Patient Information – Exercise

I. **TRUE/FALSE.**
   Mark the following true or false.

1. The number of payers listed in FL 50 may affect the number of entries in FLs 51, 52, 53, 54, 58 and 59.
   - ● true
   - ○ false

2. Codes in FL 34 only require one date to be entered with each code.
   - ● true
   - ○ false

3. When listing codes in FLs 39–41, codes that begin with letters come first.
   - ○ true
   - ● false

4. 2:21 A.M. would be coded as 02 for FLs 13 and 16.
   - ● true
   - ○ false

5. Condition codes are reported in a two-digit format.
   - ● true
   - ○ false

6. 12191977 is a proper date entry for FL 6.
   - ○ true
   - ● false

7. 12191977 is a proper date entry for FL 10.
   - ● true
   - ○ false

8. Code 3 would be used to indicate an emergency in FL 14.
   - ○ true
   - ● false

9. FLs 31–34 are to be filled out left to right before moving on to the second row.
   - ● true
   - ○ false

10. FL 29 is required for all submissions.
    - ○ true
    - ● false

II. MATCHING.
Match the correct term to the definition.

1. H   FL 10
2. B   FL 15
3. G   NUBC
4. A   FL
5. J   FL 59
6. D   UB-82
7. E   FL 8b
8. C   FL 14
9. F   UB-04
10. I   Official UB-04 Data Specifications Manual

A. Form locator
B. Used for referral source code
C. Used to code the priority of the encounter
D. The first adopted Uniform Bill
E. Used to enter the name of the patient
F. Used by facilities to bill payers today
G. National Uniform Billing Committee
H. Used to enter the patient date of birth
I. Electronic guide explaining how to complete the UB-04
J. Used to show the relationship of patient to the insured

Healthcare Provider Information – Lesson 1

For third-party payers to have a complete picture of the services they are being billed for, they must also have some detailed information about the healthcare providers who delivered the services.

There are several form locators devoted to reporting the details of the healthcare provider. We will go through these and illustrate their proper use.

FL 1 is one of the most conspicuous locators on the entire UB-04 form. It is a large box divided into 4 equal lines and it contains no heading. This is the space for the healthcare provider submitting the claim form to the payer to enter their name, address, and telephone number. These are to be entered without punctuation, and no punctuation or spaces are used in the telephone number, as seen below:

1 Shady Oak Nursing Home	2	3a PAT. CNTL #	2345179612		
117 Elm Ave		b. MED. REC. #	151236		
Lincoln WV 7772		5 FED. TAX NO.	6 STATEMENT COVERS PERIOD	FROM	THROUGH
1115552389		17-6145178		101206	101206

FL 2 is used if the healthcare provider needs payment to be sent to an address other than that listed in item 1. If this is not used, it should be left blank.

Since we have already covered FLs 3 and 4, let's skip down to FL 5.

FL 5 is reserved for the employer's identification number (often referred to as the EIN). This is the tax identification number that the IRS assigns to nearly all businesses. When this number is being entered electronically, the hyphen used in the number should not be entered.

We will now skip all the way down to FL 56.

FL 56 is another unique identifier assigned to the healthcare provider. When the HIPAA rule was enacted, one of the provisions was the creation of the National Plan and Provider Enumeration System to assign unique identifying numbers to all healthcare providers. The purpose was to use the numbers to more accurately and efficiently transfer healthcare information (like all of the information on the UB-04) electronically.

Healthcare Provider Information – Lesson 2

FL 57 is used for identifying numbers that third-party payers assign to the providers for their own use. You'll notice that there are three available lines in this form locator. The numbers should align with the proper third-party payer from FL 50.

We will now go all the way down to FL 76.

FL 76 is used to identify the attending physician (inpatient) or the ordering physician (outpatient). You will notice there is a place for the physician's NPI number. The space to the right of the NPI is used for entering the physician's qualifying codes. The first box has room for two characters. These are used to identify what type of secondary identifier will follow (1G=Provider Unique Physician Identification Number; G2=Provider's commercial number; 0B=Physician's license number from licensing state). The number that follows in the box to the right can then be matched to the proper type of identifier.

The line below the identifying numbers is for the physician's last name and first name (all caps).

FL 77 is used to identify the physician who performed a medical procedure (if one was performed). The format is the same as FL 76.

FLs 78 and 79 are used to identify any other physicians who had roles in the care provided. The NUBC Official Data Specifications Manual has codes listed that are used to identify the type or role of individual physicians listed in these FLs. That code is entered into the first blank next to the word *other*. The remaining spaces are to be completed in the same manner as FLs 76 and 77.

50 PAYER NAME	51 HEALTH PLAN ID	52 REL INFO	53 ASG BEN	54 PRIOR PAYMENTS	55 EST. AMOUNT DUE	56 NPI	7811654831
IHC	678	Y	Y			57 OTHER PRV ID	678143

58 INSURED'S NAME	59 P.REL	60 INSURED'S UNIQUE ID	61 GROUP NAME	62 INSURANCE GROUP NO.
Jackson John	18	AAAA123666173		782153

63 TREATMENT AUTHORIZATION CODES	64 DOCUMENT CONTROL NUMBER	65 EMPLOYER NAME

66 DX: 600.00 788.1

69 ADMIT DX: 600.00   70 PATIENT REASON DX   71 PPS CODE   72 ECI

74 PRINCIPAL PROCEDURE CODE/DATE

76 ATTENDING NPI 6137251732 QUAL G2
LAST Jones   FIRST John

77 OPERATING NPI QUAL
78 OTHER NPI QUAL
79 OTHER NPI QUAL

UB-04 CMS-1450   APPROVED OMB NO. 0938-0997   NUBC National Uniform Billing Committee   THE CERTIFICATIONS ON THE REVERSE APPLY TO THIS BILL AND ARE MADE A PART HEREOF.

With that we are finished with the Healthcare Provider information portions of the UB-04. Let's take a break for a giggle before we move onto the last group of form locators.

Medical Humor

A lady was being seen by her doctor when he took a deep breath and sighed. "I hate to say it, but that knee's going to need reconstructive surgery."

The lady, incredulous, lifted an eyebrow and said, "I think I want a second opinion."

The doctor replied, "Okay...in that case, a face lift might be a good idea."

I. MULTIPLE CHOICE.
Choose the best answer.

1. FL 2 is completed _____.
   - ○ always
   - ● only if the provider needs payments to be sent to an alternate address
   - ○ for providers to duplicate their business address
   - ○ only if the provider has international offices

2. FL 5 has a space for the EIN. This number is _____.
   - ● assigned by the IRS
   - ○ optional
   - ○ always hyphenated
   - ○ used to provide information about the provider's history

3. FL 57 is used for identifying numbers _____.
   ○ for each physician
   ○ that indicate providers' physical locations
   ● assigned by the third-party payer
   ○ for outpatient providers only

4. FL 1 requires _____.
   ● no punctuation
   ○ an identifying number
   ○ an attached document
   ○ all of the above

5. FL 56 is _____.
   ○ the same as the number entered in FL 57
   ● is used for a number assigned by the National Plan and Provider Enumeration System
   ○ filled in if the provider being used is based outside of the United States
   ○ optional

Healthcare Services Information – Lesson 1

The last group of form locators we will go through are those dealing with the encounter and the services provided. These will detail to the third-party payer exactly what the diagnoses were and what care was given. With this information, the payer will have a complete picture of the who, what, where, when, why, and how of the entire encounter...all scrunched onto one page. It's pretty impressive how much information is contained in this one small form.

We are now to the point where we get to address the largest FLs in the UB-04.

FLs 42 and 43 need to be addressed together because they are both doing the same thing—documenting the revenue codes. **Revenue codes** are extensive and they are listed in full in the NUBC Official Data Specifications Manual. They are used to describe services rendered during treatment. They are done differently for inpatient and outpatient encounters. Inpatient revenue codes will bundled under an umbrella that covers all associated services. Outpatient revenue codes are itemized and listed separately for each service. FL 42 is used to record the four-digit code itself. The codes are divided into categories by the first three digits and the last digit is a variable that gives specific details of the service. Let's look at the revenue codes for renal dialysis services:

0800 Renal Dialysis

0801 Hemodialysis
0802 Peritoneal dialysis
0803 CAPD
0804 CCPD
0809 Other inp dialysis

The revenue code 0800 is used for renal dialysis, with the final zero denoting a "general" code. Many payers require a more detailed 4th code. You'll notice in the list above that the fourth digit is the only part of the code that differs and each fourth digit provides more information about the renal dialysis.

Revenue codes are vast and varied, ranging from room and board codes to anesthesia codes to pharmacy codes.

Line 22 of this locator must be filled in with revenue code 0001, total charge. This line will be used to calculate the total charge once FLs 42–49 are entered.

FL 43 is used to give a shortened description of the revenue code (notice the descriptions in the example above). Most software programs used for entering revenue codes will populate FL 43 automatically when you enter the numeric code in FL 42.

There are 22 total spaces in FLs 42 and 43 and the codes you list should be entered numerically, beginning with the smallest number and working to the greatest number.

FL 44 has three distinct headers: "HCPCS/Accommodation Rates/HIPPS." The type of revenue code listed will determine which of these codes will be used. If the bill is for an outpatient procedure, the appropriate HCPCS code must be listed. For outpatient services, procedures done more than once will be listed in FL 42 as many times as they were performed. The corresponding HCPCS code will be listed by each entry. If a HCPCS code is available for an inpatient code, it must be listed here.

HIPPS codes are codes developed for providers based on historical data to indicate specific details about a revenue code. Individual third-party payers may use these codes and it will be up to the biller to correspond with payers and maintain up-to-date knowledge of HIPPS codes.

Accommodation rates refer to inpatient bills and give detailed information about the patient's stay.

FL 45 is used for outpatient services. The date the service was rendered is entered for each of the revenue codes and is listed in the MMDDYY format. These are generally not required for inpatient services.

At the bottom of this column, you will see a space for "Creation date." Enter the date the bill is created in this space using the same format for the date.

FL 46 is used to denote the units "used" in the revenue code. Revenue codes represent a wide variety of services so the units represented can mean many things. The number of days may be entered for an accommodation code, but for different codes, the unit number could represent the number of times a patient was treated or a metric measurement of fluids.

FL 47 is used to record the total charge for the revenue code. If the service units are more than one, the charge would be multiplied by that number. For instance, if an inpatient bill states that a pediatric patient remained for 5 nights, the charge for revenue code 0123 would be multiplied by five to get the total reported in FL 47.

At the bottom of this column, the total charges will be entered into line 22 and
The box below titled "Totals."

FL 48 is titled "non-covered charges." This is used to record monetary amounts of charges that are not covered by the third-party payer or those that are not deemed reasonable for the type of care being given.

FL 49 is not used at this time and may be used in the future for additional codes.

FL 55 is not required by all third-party payers. This is where the total charges the provider is expecting to be paid is recorded.

I. **TRUE/FALSE.**
   Mark the following true or false.

   1. Since FL 49 is not used "N/A" should be entered in this space.
      ○ true
      ● false

   2. A proper FL 45 entry would be 091971.
      ● true
      ○ false

   3. The units recorded in FL 46 always represent days.
      ○ true
      ● false

   4. FL 44 may contain a HCPCS code.
      ● true
      ○ false

   5. FL 48 is used only for elective surgeries.
      ○ true
      ● false

Healthcare Services Information – Lesson 2

Let's now skip down to FL 66, our next "blank" form locator.

FL 66 is used to report the International Classification of Diseases codebook being used to report the diagnosis codes. Since the U.S. has not yet adopted the ICD-10, you will enter 9 (for ICD-9) in this space.

FL 67 is unique in appearance and use. You'll notice that the number 67 is watermarked in the background of the first space and then there are consecutive spaces lettered A–Q. The locator marked 67 is used to record the principal ICD-9 diagnosis code and a special code used for denoting the status of the diagnosis at the time of admission (referred to as present on admission or POA). The principal diagnosis code (a 3-digit code) would have the POA tacked on in the fourth digit position. The POA codes are as follows:

Code	POA
Y	Diagnosis was present at time of admission.
N	Diagnosis was not present at time of admission.
U	Documentation does not indicate whether diagnosis was present at time of admission.
W	Physician was unable to determine whether diagnosis was present at time of admission.
1	The reported diagnosis code does not require a POA code.

The subsequent A–Q spaces are used to report codes for any additional conditions that the patient may have had on admission or may have acquired during treatment.

FL 68 is to be left blank at this time. It may be used in the future for recording information.

FL 69 is used to report the ICD-9 diagnosis code that is the reason for admission (for inpatient treatment). The reason for admission/condition is determined by the official ICD-9-CM coding Guidelines.

FL 70 has 3 lettered spaces (a–c) for reporting the codes for the diagnoses responsible for the patient's initial visit. This FL is used to code ICD-9 codes for outpatient visits only. These codes will give the payer the reason for the patient's visit, which can affect payment.

FL 71, while small, is important to reimbursement and can be complicated. Many providers have contracts with third-party payers that outline payment of procedures through a prospective payment system. These codes, known as diagnostic related groups (DRGs), encompass a variety of resources and compile them into a single code with a single charge. The last unit of this module will explain in detail how to arrive at the proper DRG code.

FL 72 has spaces for 3 codes. Here you report the external cause of injury codes (if there are any). These are codes are mandatory when a patient has been injured, poisoned, or suffered an adverse effect. These codes also use the present on admission modifiers that were used in FL 67.

FL 73 is to be left blank at this time. It may be used in the future for recording information.

FL 74 is used to report the principal ICD-9 procedure code. The box beside the code is reserved for the date the procedure was performed. There are also duplicate spaces A–E that are used for other procedures that may have been performed.

FL 75 is to be left blank at this time. It may be used in the future for recording information.

FL 80 is the last remaining form locator (hooray!). We have said all along that the purpose of the UB-04 is to transform complex healthcare documentation into alphanumeric form for processing. The codes make adjudication and payment more efficient and accurate. However, the nature of our language is that our narratives cannot be represented with complete accuracy by codes. FL 80 allows for a provider to enter comments that they feel were not represented in the codes or that will make the claim form more accurate and complete when the payer is evaluating it. This is not mandatory.

After all of those codes, dates, lists, modifiers, how about a little laugh?

Medical Humor

Phil went to the doctor, who happened to be his best friend Dave. He had a stomachache and Dr. Dave checked him out thoroughly. After the exam, Phil said, "Dave, I know my money is no good here, but I just want you to know that yesterday I revised my will and you are now included in it."

Dr. Dave grabbed the prescription back from Phil and said, "In that case, let me revise this prescription."

Unit 6
Reimbursement Methodologies

Reimbursement Methodologies – Introduction

How's your memory? Do you remember way back in the Healthcare Structure and Organization module when you studied the major players in the healthcare scene in the United States? Or do you barely remember what you had for breakfast? We figure you are a lot like us (what was for breakfast?) and a little memory refreshment is probably a good idea.

In Healthcare Structure and Organization, you learned the United States has a first-party and third-party payer system; a patient directly reimburses the healthcare provider (first-party payer) for healthcare services or the patient has secured coverage from another source (third-party payer) that reimburses some or all of the cost of a patient's healthcare services.

Patient reimburses healthcare provider for services = first-party payer

Entity other than the patient reimburses provider for services = third-party payer

Let's dust off the list of third-party payers:

- Government
- Group/Individual Insurers
- Industrial/Workers' Compensation
- Automobile Insurers
- Liability Insurers

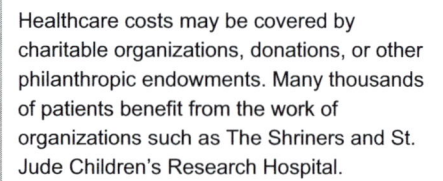

Highlights

Healthcare costs may be covered by charitable organizations, donations, or other philanthropic endowments. Many thousands of patients benefit from the work of organizations such as The Shriners and St. Jude Children's Research Hospital.

We will be referring to third-party payers in the upcoming lessons, so if you are feeling a little rusty, review the third-party payer section of the Healthcare Structure and Organization module. Information is summarized on a couple of charts back there a module or two (or five).

Is this starting to sound at least vaguely familiar? Good—because we are going to explore reimbursement methodologies used by payers in the healthcare reimbursement system.

Reimbursement in the Healthcare Environment

In the previous unit, you learned the healthcare providers' process for billing for services. In this unit, you will learn reimbursement methodologies used by first and third-party payers to determine how much is *actually paid* for healthcare services.

In the last unit you learned healthcare providers set fees (fee schedule/chargemaster) for their services. Fees are based on a number of variables, including labor costs, professional credentials, malpractice insurance, competition, and the cost of office space and equipment. As you can imagine, the cost of office space in San Francisco is significantly higher than in Cheyenne, Wyoming; this would be reflected in higher-than-average healthcare provider costs for San Francisco compared to those for Cheyenne. All of these factors (and many not listed) are considerations for healthcare providers as they set charges/fees for services. However, healthcare providers often don't collect the same amount they charge.

Complex contractual relationships exist between patient, government, third–party payers, and providers.

If healthcare operated like a large retail store, providers would set the prices based on costs and the competition in their area of service; patients would come in and choose whether to purchase goods and services. If they decided to purchase, a bill would be presented, paid (by the patient or third-party payer), and the patient would go on his or her merry way.

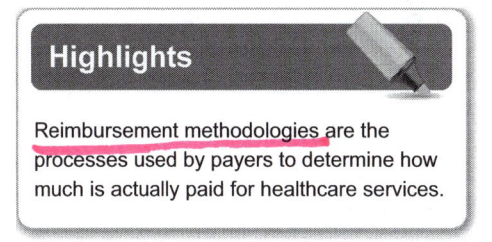

Highlights

Reimbursement methodologies are the processes used by payers to determine how much is actually paid for healthcare services.

Why doesn't the healthcare industry operate like this?

There are four key reasons why healthcare reimbursement is different from other types of consumer purchases:

- The consumer of healthcare services (patient) is often not the person who pays for healthcare goods/services.
- Complex contractual relationships exist between patient, government, third-party payers, and providers.
- The dollar amount actually collected by the provider for a service may vary widely depending on who pays for the service.
- The government is the largest single payer of healthcare services, and the amount they pay is not governed by the price charged but by reimbursement rules and regulations based on laws.

The Consumer

☑ **The consumer of healthcare services (patient) is often not the person who pays for healthcare goods/services.**

In some cases in the healthcare world, consumers pay for their healthcare as they would anything else-- they are charged for a service performed, and pay it from their own pockets. Of course, that can get expensive very quickly, and much of the time a third-party payer is used.

Let's go back a few years to the early days of third-party payers. Imagine you wanted to go shopping or enjoy a weeklong vacation and you had a gift certificate with virtually no price limit. Would your buying habits be different than if you knew you had to pay the bill? Probably yes. Would you enjoy a little more room service or pamper yourself with a nicer hotel with added extras? Probably yes. Would value and price be a primary consideration in your choices? Probably not!

For many years, the healthcare model operated much like this. The patient had insurance and visited the healthcare provider. The provider presented a bill to the insurance company who then paid the bill. The provider and the patient did not have much incentive to keep costs low or restrict the scope of services as much as possible.

What happened? Government and private insurance providers rebelled. Third-party payers wanted more control over what the patient could choose and what the provider could provide if they were going to pay the bill. Third-party payers began to look seriously at ways of "managing" what services the patient could access and under what conditions they could access them. Third-party payers also began to look seriously at ways of incentivizing healthcare providers to work with them to control spiraling healthcare costs.

I. **TRUE/FALSE.**
   Mark the following true or false.

   1. For many years, people struggled to pay their own medical bills before insurance agencies and the government stepped in to help.

      ○ true
      ● false

   2. The consumer of healthcare services always pays directly for healthcare goods and services.

      ○ true
      ● false

   3. Third-party payers eventually began to manage what services the patient could access and under what conditions they could access them.

      ● true
      ○ false

Governmental Controls

The third-party payer system began to undergo significant change. Healthcare providers could no longer set prices and expect to receive dollar for dollar payment. By changing insurance contracts with patients and entering into contractual relationships with providers, third-party payers began to restrict and "manage" healthcare relationships between providers and patients.

Today there are several managed-care models and strategies employed by third-party payers to manage healthcare costs.

What about government? Government doesn't go out and sell insurance through employers or private policies. Government is the third-party payer for special demographic groups of Americans, such as veterans, indigenous people, the disabled, and the poor. Individuals who qualify for government-sponsored healthcare services prove they fit the requirements for the government-sponsored program and they receive healthcare benefits.

Government puts price and choice control pressure on healthcare providers through rules and regulations mandating reimbursement based on systems other than the traditional payment of provider-set rates.

> **Highlights**
>
> Employers often are the purchasers of healthcare insurance, which they then pass on to employees in employer-sponsored healthcare plans. Insurance companies began to change coverage options available to employers, making options with managed-care features more financially attractive.

> **Highlights**
>
> Medicare is the only government program considered to be health insurance. Medicare is defined as insurance because Medicare premiums are withheld from the paychecks of working Americans and used to fund the Medicare program.

In the future we will discuss government reimbursement methodologies in more detail.

Contract Relationships

Healthcare reimbursement methodologies are different from traditional market systems:

- ☑ **Complex contractual relationships exist between patient, government, third-party payers, and providers.**

Healthcare purchases are not straight buy-the-goods, pay-the-bill two-party transactions. High healthcare costs add layers of complexity to the healthcare transaction, requiring the said contract relationships.

> **Highlights**
>
> Blue Cross and Blue Shield began the healthcare reimbursement revolution in the 1920s by contracting with Baylor University to provide a fixed hospitalization rate for Dallas school teachers of $6.00 per day for up to 21 days.*
>
> *http://eh.net/encyclopedia

Prior to Blue Cross and Blue Shield in the 1920s and 1930s, virtually all reimbursement was between patient and provider. The most common form of payment was first-party payer. If individuals had insurance at all, it was "sickness" insurance and not health insurance. Sickness insurance paid the employee for work time lost from being sick so he/she could pay medical bills; this system did not involve direct payment to healthcare providers.

In the 1920s, Blue Cross and Blue Shield introduced the revolutionary concept of negotiated reimbursement rates for insured patients—and there was no turning back. Keep in mind the 1920s and 1930s also marked a period of explosive advances in healthcare research with resulting leaps forward in advanced treatment options and (of course) costs.

The period between 1940 and 1960 saw explosive growth in the ranks of the insured patient—from 20 million in 1940 to 142 million in the 1950s. This ushered in the decades of spiraling healthcare costs and the desire of insurers to take a more active role in managing healthcare reimbursement.

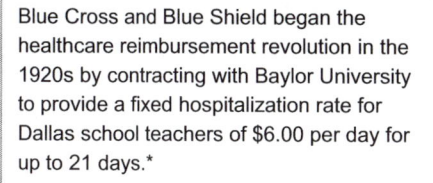

I. **TRUE/FALSE.**
   Mark the following true or false.

   1. Blue Cross and Blue Shield began the healthcare reimbursement revolution.
      - ● true
      - ○ false

   2. All medical payments were between the patient and the provider until the healthcare reimbursement revolution in the 1920's and 1930's.
      - ● true
      - ○ false

   3. Healthcare purchases are usually very straightforward two-party transactions.
      - ○ true
      - ● false

Payment

Today, relationships between patient, provider, government, and private-third party payers range in complexity from uninsured patients paying as they access healthcare services to insurance companies owning healthcare provider networks where their insured are treated at vastly reduced rates.

The intricate relationships between payer, patient, and provider lead to the third reason healthcare reimbursement structures are complex.

> ✓ **The dollar amount actually collected by the provider for a service may vary widely depending on who pays for the service.**

When the patient pays, the transaction is often dollar for dollar. The patient pays the amount billed for the service with the use of cash, credit, or payment plans. The provider may offer discounts for payment at the time of service or assist the patient in setting up payment plans or applying for loans.

Self-pay example

Fred is a self-pay patient of Dr. Tony Gates. Fred was examined by Dr. Gates for fever, sore throat, and cough. Dr. Gates performed a rapid strep test.

DR. GATES'S CHARGES			PRIVATE PAY	
CODE	DESCRIPTION	CHARGE	CODE	REIMBURSEMENT
99213	EXAM	$85.00	99213	$85.00
87880	STREP TEST	$15.00	87880	$15.00

Fred pays $20 at the counter as he leaves the office. He pays the balance of $80 by check after he receives his statement in the mail.

On the other hand, third-party relationships may result in the healthcare provider collecting less than the billed amount for services.

Insurance example

Elaine had been seen by Dr. Tony Gates six weeks ago because she had a fever, sore throat, and cough. The office billed her insurance carrier, United Health Care, and received the following reimbursement:

DR. GATES'S CHARGES			UNITED HEALTH CARE REIMBURSEMENT	
CODE	DESCRIPTION	CHARGE	CODE	REIMBURSEMENT
99213	EXAM	$85.00	99213	$75.75
87880	STREP TEST	$15.00	87880	$14.25

United Health Care has a contractual agreement with Dr. Gates' office. Dr. Gates accepts a negotiated lower rate as payment in full for United Health Care patients, and the balance of $10 is written off by Dr. Gates and not billed to the patient.

Government also uses reimbursement formulas that result in total payment being significantly less than the total bill.

Government example

Barb has Medicaid and was seen by Dr. Tony Gates five weeks ago for a fever, cough, and sore throat. The office billed Barb's insurance and received the following reimbursement:

DR. GATES'S CHARGES			MEDICAID REIMBURSEMENT	
CODE	DESCRIPTION	CHARGE	CODE	REIMBURSEMENT
99213	EXAM	$85.00	99213	$40.34
87880	STREP TEST	$15.00	87880	$8.74

In Barb's state, Medicaid regulations do not allow providers to collect co-payment or balances from the patient. Dr. Gates writes off the balance of $50.92.

The net effect is healthcare providers are constantly working to maintain a healthy cost/profit to amount collected ratio.

Fee: $100	Patient 1: Patient pays $100
	Patient 2: Third party payer pays $90
	Patient 3: Government pays $49.08

Average amount collected for service: $79.69

Healthcare providers must balance fees, the cost of doing business, and the reimbursement received to continue to provide healthcare services.

I. TRUE/FALSE.
Mark the following true or false.

1. Healthcare transactions are always dollar-for-dollar.
   - ○ true
   - ● false

2. Third-party relationships may mean the healthcare provider collects less than the billed amount for services
   - ● true
   - ○ false

3. The government's reimbursement formulas result in total payments being significantly less than the total bill.
   - ● true
   - ○ false

Government

☑ **The government is the largest single payer of healthcare services, and the amount they pay is not governed by the price charged but by reimbursement rules and regulations based on laws.**

The U.S. government pays for more healthcare services than any other single entity in the U.S. healthcare system. In more and more situations, the government does not base healthcare reimbursement on what is charged by healthcare providers; the government makes reimbursement determinations by applying the rules and regulations written by the various agencies administering federal and state healthcare funds. The Centers for Medicare & Medicaid (CMS), Indian Health Services (IHS), the Department of Veterans' Affairs (VA), and other government-sponsored healthcare programs each follow the reimbursement methodology mandated by law and written by their governing agencies.

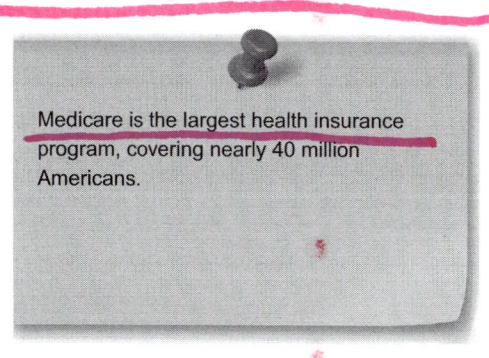

> Medicare is the largest health insurance program, covering nearly 40 million Americans.

For example, IHS uses a per diem system for outpatient physician billing where, regardless of the cost for treatment and/or complexity of the patient's condition, reimbursement is based on a per diem or per encounter rate. IHS tracks average cost per patient per day or per patient per encounter over time and, based on this history, sets a daily reimbursement rate for patients who are qualified to receive IHS benefits.

As you can easily imagine, this puts pressure on everyone else in the system. If a provider charges $100 for a service and the government standard reimbursement is only $40 for the service, the provider receives $60 less than billed for each patient. Healthcare providers may respond by A) raising prices or B) by cancelling their contract with the government third-party payer who is reimbursing the physician the lowest.

Low Medicare Physician Payment Rates Cause Patient Access Problems

Primary care physicians are already scarce in Alaska, but recently it has become even more difficult for Alaskan Medicare beneficiaries to see a doctor. The Anchorage Daily News reports that Medicare reimbursement rates in Alaska have dropped below half of a physician's customary and reasonable visit fee. Physicians estimate that they cannot continue to operate a practice if more than 25% of their patients have Medicare, as opposed to private insurance coverage. Many refuse to see patients with Medicare altogether. This problem has arisen first in Alaska because it costs more to practice medicine in Alaska than elsewhere in the U.S. However, some experts predict that it will become a more widespread issue if Medicare physician payments are not increased.

(About.com. http://healthinsurance.about.com/?once=true&)

I. **TRUE/FALSE.**
   Mark the following true or false.

   1. The largest health insurance program is Medicare.
      - ● true
      - ○ false

   2. The U.S. government bases healthcare reimbursement on what is charged by healthcare providers.
      - ○ true
      - ● false

   3. Healthcare providers may cancel their contract with the government third-party payer.
      - ● true
      - ○ false

Review: Healthcare Reimbursement

I. **MULTIPLE CHOICE.**
   Choose the best answer.

   1. There are four reasons why healthcare reimbursement is different than other types of consumer purchases. Select the statement that is NOT one of those reasons.
      - ● Government requires all payers to reimburse at the same rate for the same services.
      - ○ The patient is not always the person who pays for their healthcare services.
      - ○ Complex contractual agreements exist between patients, third-party payers, government payers and providers.
      - ○ Reimbursement/amount collected by the provider may vary greatly depending on who is paying for the service.

   2. Who is the largest single payer of healthcare costs in the United States?
      - ○ Blue Cross Blue Shield
      - ○ United Health Care
      - ○ private pay
      - ● government

   3. Today many third-party payers have turned to _____ to control healthcare costs.
      - ○ the government
      - ○ other third-party payers
      - ● managed-care coverage
      - ○ discount insurance carriers

4. Healthcare providers bill for services from a chargemaster or fee schedule. Prices for services are based on a variety of factors. Which of the following would NOT be a consideration for developing a fee schedule?
   - ○ competition and labor costs
   - ○ price of malpractice insurance
   - ○ labor and office space costs
   - ● patient ethnicity

5. Third-party payers make managed care more attractive to employers by offering _____ for selecting healthcare plans with more managed care features.
   - ○ lifetime coverage
   - ● lower premiums (rates)
   - ○ extended payment plans
   - ○ minimized coding efforts

Healthcare Reimbursement Methodologies

We've walked through a high-level discussion of why healthcare reimbursement is a horse of a different color from the standard goods/services purchase. You've seen a few real examples of how private and government third-party payers approach reimbursement.

Let's focus now on specific types of healthcare reimbursement methodologies by building a healthcare reimbursement methodologies chart. You should keep a couple of important thoughts in mind as you work through the next several lessons. The various reimbursement methodologies presented do not represent a comprehensive list of all reimbursement methodologies. You will be exposed to the most common methodologies you are likely to encounter in the workplace. In addition, you will encounter a lot of terms and definitions related to healthcare reimbursement methodologies. Don't let all of the terms confuse you. Take them one by one. Study the term, the definition, and the examples until you feel you could describe the reimbursement methodology to your friend, your spouse, or someone else who would be willing to listen to you ramble on about healthcare reimbursement.

Fee-For-Service and Episode-of-Care

Healthcare reimbursement methodologies breakdown into two primary types:

Fee-For-Service
Episode-of-Care

In a fee-for-service reimbursement system, the provider receives payment for each service provided to the patient. The amount of reimbursement is determined by reviewing the services received by the patient. In other words, determination is based on "what was done" for the patient and not "what was wrong" with the patient.

In a fee-for-service reimbursement system, reimbursement is based on what services are provided to the patient.

Dr. Derek Shepherd's office sent in a claim to Aetna Insurance for Bob's date of service six weeks ago for the following charges, and the office has received the following reimbursement:

DR. SHEPHERD'S CHARGES			AETNA'S REIMBURSEMENT	
CODE	DESCRIPTION	CHARGE	CODE	PAYMENT
99214	Exam	$110.00	99214	$95.68
71010	2-view chest x-ray	$95.00	71010	$81.73

Episode-of-care is a reimbursement system under which physician-based providers receive reimbursement based on the length of time for which the patient is treated. This is usually in reference to situations such as surgery, a minor procedure, or a long-term treatment such as dialysis. The amount of reimbursement is determined by reviewing the unit of time the patient is treated and then makes payment. Payments are based on "what was done" and in the case of a surgical procedure; it includes a "global package." The global package is either 10 or 90 days of care after the surgery where the patient does not pay for an office visit pertaining to the surgery.

Under an episode-of-care reimbursement system, reimbursement is based on the patient's particular condition/illness or a specified time period over which the patient receives care.

Lorraine, a 75-year-old woman, had a total hip replacement performed four weeks ago. She is in today to see Dr. Shepherd for a follow-up visit from her surgery. Medicare was billed $3,500.00. Medicare reimbursed Dr. Shepherd $1,216.49. Lorraine's office visit's charge for today is 0.00 because it is included in the charged amount for the hip replacement.

Fee-For-Service
Reimbursement based on:
Services provided to the patient

Episode-of-Care
Reimbursement based on:
Patient's condition/illness
A specified time period

You are going to learn about three fee-for-service models and three episode-of-care models.

Fee-For-Service	Episode-of-Care
1. Self-pay 2. Retrospective payment 3. Managed care	1. Managed care – capitation 2. Global payment/Prospective payment 3. Prospective payment

I. **TRUE/FALSE.**
   Mark the following true or false.

   1. Healthcare reimbursement methodologies are based on only one model.
      - ○ true
      - ● false

   2. Fee-for-service systems determine reimbursement based on what was done for the patient rather than what was wrong with the patient.
      - ● true
      - ○ false

   3. In episode-of-care, reimbursement is based on the patient's illness or an amount of time over which the patient is cared for.
      - ● true
      - ○ false

Self-Pay

Reimbursement based on:
Services provided to the patient

   ☑ 1. Self-pay
   2. Retrospective payment
   3. Managed care

Patients without third-party payer coverage or with very restrictive third-party coverage pay for healthcare services on a fee-for-service basis. The patient seeks healthcare services, receives a bill itemizing services received, and makes payment directly to the provider. Payment options for self-pay patients vary depending on the policies of the healthcare provider. Some providers will not see patients who do not have insurance coverage without payment in full at the time of service. Other providers offer options for monthly payment plans.

Self-Pay Example 1

Suzanne is a self-pay patient of Dr. Meredith Grey. Suzanne came into the office with complaints of hives and itching. She was examined by Dr. Grey; she gave Suzanne an injection of Benadryl 50 mg IM for the itching and hives. The patient went to the front desk to check out and pay her bill. Her charges were:

DR. GREY'S CHARGES			SUZANNE'S PAYMENT WITH DEBIT CARD	
CODE	DESCRIPTION	CHARGE	CODE	PAYMENT
99212	Exam	$65.00	99212	$65.00
J1200	Benadryl 50 mg	$15.00	J1200	$15.00

Self-Pay w/Discount Example 2

Simon came in to see Dr. Christina Yang today for heart palpitations and dizziness. Dr. Yang performed an exam and an EKG. Simon went to the front desk to check out. Dr. Yang is giving him a 5% discount if he pays in full today, something he offers all his patients. Dr. Yang's charges are:

DR. YANG'S CHARGES			SIMON'S PAYMENT WITH DEBIT CARD		
CODE	DESCRIPTION	CHARGE	CODE	DISCOUNT	PAYMENT
99213	Exam	$75.00	99213	$3.75	$71.25
93000	EKG	$50.00	93000	$2.50	$47.50

Payer with Private Policy Reimbursement Example 3

Laura, a 45-year-old, is a patient of Dr. Derek Shepherd. She was seen eight weeks ago for a routine physical, EKG, and urinalysis. Laura is not technically a self-pay patient since she has Beech Street Insurance through a private policy she has purchased herself. However, Dr. Shepherd does not participate with her insurance. So, Laura paid her bill in full at the time of service and received an itemized statement to send to Beech Street for reimbursement. Here are the charges submitted and Beech Street's reimbursement to Laura.

DR. SHEPHERD'S CHARGES			BEECH STREET'S REIMBURSEMENT TO PATIENT	
99396	Routine Physical	$115.00	99396	$100.00
93000	EKG	$50.00	93000	$45.00
81000	Urinalysis	$10.00	81000	$5.00

Patients without third-party health insurance who do not qualify for benefits under a government health program are on the rise in the United States. With the high cost of healthcare, many self-pay patients find their healthcare options limited when they cannot pay for the services they need.

I. **FILL IN THE BLANK.**
   Enter the correct word in the blank provided.

   1. Many _Self-pay_ patients find their options for healthcare are limited when they are unable to pay for needed services.

   2. Patients without _third-party payer_ coverage pay for healthcare on a fee-for-service basis.

   3. _Payment Options_ for self-pay patients vary depending on the policies of the individual healthcare provider.

Retrospective Payment

Reimbursement based on:
Services provided to the patient

   1. Self-pay
   ☑ 2. Retrospective payment
   3. Managed care

Self-pay is a form of retrospective payment, but traditionally retrospective payment systems are discussed in terms of third-party payers.

> **Retrospective: Review of past events**
> When a patient receives healthcare services and reimbursement is determined based on past events, this is called a **retrospective payment system.**

As with all fee-for-service reimbursement methodologies, retrospective payment systems make payment based on services rendered ("what was done" for the patient) and not based on "what was wrong" with the patient or "how long" the patient was treated. Retrospective payment systems are called retrospective because payment is based on costs or charges actually incurred for the care of the patient during his or her healthcare encounter. Payment decisions are made after the costs are incurred (retrospectively).

Self-pay patients usually pay the full amount for services rendered. Under traditional retrospective payment systems, third-party payers can pay the full amount of the services rendered, but more often they negotiate a discounted fee-for-service system. Under a discounted fee-for-service retrospective payment system, the third-party payer pays less than the full price charged for the service. Depending on the contractual agreement(s) between provider, third-party payer, and patient, the difference between the price charged and the amount paid by the third-party payer may or may not be passed on to the patient. In other words, the discount gained by the third-party payer doesn't necessarily have to be passed on to the patient.

I. **FILL IN THE BLANK.**
   Enter the correct word in the blank provided.

   1. Retrospective payment is based on _costs or charges_ actually incurred for the care of the patient.

   2. Payment decisions are made _after_ the costs are incurred.

   3. In retrospective payment, the third-party payer pays _less than_ the full price charged for the service.

Fee Schedules

Fee schedules are a discounted fee-for-service system used by many third-party payers to establish maximum reimbursement rates (also known as allowable fees). Third-party payers establish a fee schedule that lists all services and the maximum allowable rate the insurer will pay. When the provider sends the claim to the third-party payer, reimbursement is based on the service provided but not at the provider's rate. The reimbursement rate is based on the third-party payer's fee schedule for that service.

CODE	DESCRIPTION	PROVIDER FEE	THIRD-PARTY FEE
99214	Exam	$110.00	$90.75
93000	EKG	$55.00	$48.39
81000	Urinalysis	$10.00	$8.10
71010	2-view chest x-ray	$90.00	$80.50

The provider sends a claim for an exam for $110.00 and the third-party (insurer) pays $90.75 based on their fee schedule. The balance of $19.25 may be billed to the patient by the provider or may be written off by the provider depending on the contractual relationships between the provider, the third-party payer, and the patient.

Sample Explanation of Benefits for reimbursement based on fee schedules:

> **Highlights**
>
> The difference between what is billed on a claim and what is paid by the third-party payer (the balance) is sometimes billed to the patient by the provider and sometimes written off by the provider.

Example 1

Patient Name: Adam Mitchell   Patient Acct #: 251761

Member ID # 321657415

Relation: Child   Member: Janet Mitchell

Service Dates	CPT Codes	PL	Num SVC	Submitted Charges	Copay Amount	Not Payable	See Remarks	Deduct	Co-Ins	Patient Responsible	Payable Amount
2/12/XX	22808	21	1	$2,500.00		$425.68	212				$2074.32
TOTALS				$2,500.00		$425.68					$2074.32

Remark codes 212 - Maximum allowable rate for service

For Questions regarding this claim call 888-997-4188 for assistance. Please use ID number for reference to this claim

Total Patient Responsibility _____

Explanation of Benefits shows the insurance company will pay charges up to their maximum allowable rate based on their fee schedule. The insurance company does not assign patient responsibility to the balance, so it is the provider's decision to bill or not bill the patient for the balance.

Example 2

Patient Name: Barney Rubble Patient Acct #: 197581

Member ID # 992556630

Relation: Self Member: Barney Rubble

Service Dates	CPT Codes	PL	Num SVC	Submitted Charges	Copay Amount	Not Payable	See Remarks	Deduct	Co-Ins	Patient Responsible	Payable Amount
08/04/XX	99213	11	1	$65.00	$15.00					$15.00	$50.00
08/04/XX	89247	11	1	$15.00		$8.35	325				$6.65
TOTALS				$80.00	$15.00	$8.35				$15.00	$56.65

Remark codes 325 - This is a contractual adjustment for this CPT code; do not bill the patient for this amount.

For Questions regarding this claim call 888-697-9356 for assistance. Please use ID number for reference to this claim

Total Patient Responsibility $15.00

The insurance company has a contract with the provider to pay a lesser amount than the provider's charged fee for the service. The provider cannot collect the difference between the charged amount and the discounted paid amount. The provider can only collect the patient's co-pay amount.

Example 3

Patient Name: Alan Jackson Jr. Patient Acct #: 257141

Member ID # 888569452

Relation: Child Member: Alan Jackson

Service Dates	CPT Codes	PL	Num SVC	Submitted Charges	Copay Amount	Not Payable	See Remarks	Deduct	Co-Ins	Patient Responsible	Payable Amount
08/05/XX	99213	11	1	$65.00	$20.00					$20.00	$45.00
08/05/XX	71020	11	1	$95.00		$52.41	185				$42.59
TOTALS				$160.00	$20.00	$52.41				$20.00	$87.59

Remark codes 185 - Contractual adjustment; participating physician discount.

For Questions regarding this claim call 888-551-9689 for assistance. Please use ID number for reference to this claim

Total Patient Responsibility $20.00

Once again, the insurance company and provider have a contractual relationship where the provider agrees to accept the insurer's fee schedule payment as payment in full. The provider cannot collect the difference from the patient; the provider collects only the patient's co-pay (set by the insurance company).

Usual, Customary, and Reasonable Reimbursement

The usual, customary, and reasonable reimbursement methodology is an extension of the fee schedule retrospective reimbursement system. Fee schedules are set rates for services. Usual, customary, and reasonable takes the set rate concept one step further. Usual, customary, and reasonable reimbursement rates are set by the third-party payer based on historical data for a given geographical area or a given medical specialty. Third-party payers then pay claims at the "usual, customary, and reasonable" rate and not necessarily at the billed rate.

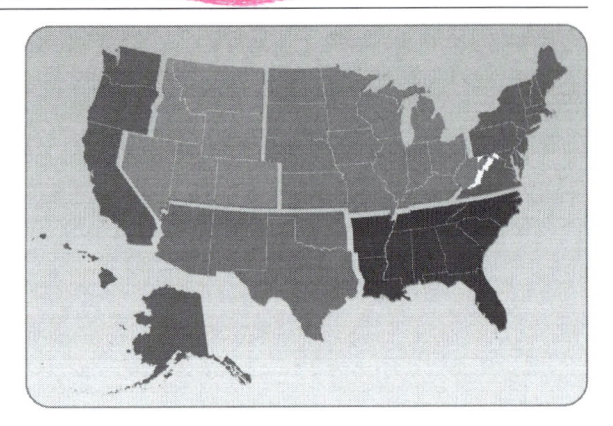

Sample Third-Party Payer Usual, Customary, and Reasonable Fee Schedules Based on Costs by Geographic Area.

CODE	SERVICE DESCRIPTION/ NORTHWEST AREA	CHARGE	USUAL/CUSTOMARY REIMBURSEMENT NORTHWEST AREA
99213	Mid-level exam	$85.00	$61.21
99214	Detailed exam	$100.00	$92.07
99215	Comprehensive exam	$135.00	$124.16
58150	Total Abdominal Hysterectomy	$1,400.00	$910.06

CODE	SERVICE DESCRIPTION/ MIDWEST AREA	CHARGE	USUAL/CUSTOMARY REIMBURSEMENT MIDWEST AREA
99213	Mid-level exam	$75.00	$64.97
99214	Detailed exam	$125.00	$97.38
99215	Comprehensive exam	$140.00	$131.99
58150	Total Abdominal Hysterectomy	$1,200.00	$1,033.17

CODE	SERVICE DESCRIPTION/ SOUTHEAST AREA	CHARGE	USUAL/CUSTOMARY REIMBURSEMENT SOUTHEAST AREA
99213	Mid-level exam	$85.00	$65.52
99214	Detailed exam	$110.00	$98.95
99215	Comprehensive exam	$140.00	$134.48
58150	Total Abdominal Hysterectomy	$1,500.00	$1,102.59

With usual, customary, and reasonable fee-for-service reimbursement, the balance may or may not be billed to the patient. Usual, customary, and reasonable retrospective payment systems may be based on geographical areas, urban versus rural, medical specialty, or other factors. Explanation of benefits often describes the difference between the amount billed by the provider and the amount paid as "over usual, customary, and reasonable (UCR) are excluded as defined by the plan."

Above Usual, Customary, and Reasonable Example #1

Patient Name: Hilary Clifford										Patient Acct #: 358761	
Member ID # 996331887											
Relation: Self										Member: Hilary Clifford	

Service Dates	CPT Codes	PL	Num SVC	Submitted Charges	Copay Amount	Not Payable	See Remarks	Deduct	Co-Ins	Patient Responsible	Payable Amount
08/10/XX	99213		1	$65.00		$10.50	735			$10.50	$55.50
08/10/XX	71020		1	$95.00		$62.35	735			$62.35	$32.65
08/10/XX											
08/10/XX											
TOTALS				$160.00		$72.85				$72.85	$88.15

Remark codes 735 - Above usual, customary, and reasonable

For Questions regarding this claim call 888-999-6868 for assistance. Please use ID number for reference to this claim	Total Patient Responsibility $72.85

Usual, customary, and reasonable reimbursement methodology is a common reimbursement model used by third-party insurers. <u>The differences are often (but not always) billed to the patient.</u>

Review: Fee-For-Service

I. **MULTIPLE CHOICE.**
   Choose the best answer.

1. Retrospective payment is an example of what type of reimbursement methodology?
   - ● fee-for-service
   - ○ episode-of-care

2. Which reimbursement methodology reimbursement rates are set by the third-party payer based on historical data for a given geographical area or a given medical specialty?
   - ○ self-pay
   - ○ managed care
   - ● usual, customary, and reasonable
   - ○ capitation

3. Episode-of-care is a reimbursement system under which the provider receives payment based on what?
   - ○ each service provided to the patient
   - ● patient's condition or illness
   - ○ the geographical area of the visit
   - ○ the length of time patient has been insured

4. Fee schedules are an example of what type of payment system?
   - ○ prospective
   - ● retrospective

5. The _____ reimbursement system is based on the patient's condition/illness or a specified time period over which the patient receives care.
   - ● episode-of-care
   - ○ fee-for-service
   - ○ fee-for-visit
   - ○ episode-of-service

Resource-Based Relative Value Scale (RBRVS)

Particularly important in outpatient coding for physician-based care is the RBRVS method used by Medicare to reimburse physicians. RBRVS, or resource-based relative value scale, is the fee-for-service reimbursement methodology used by Medicare to determine reimbursement amounts for physician-based services.

Medicaid varies from state to state since Medicaid is a joint federal and state program. Medicaid reimbursement may be based on RBRVS or a modified RBRVS system or other state-specific reimbursement methodology.

Established in 1992, the RBRVS reimbursement system seeks to set reimbursement rates for physician services based on three primary factors:

- Physician work
- Practice expense
- Professional liability

Highlights

The secretary of CMS must make available to Medicare Payment Advisory Commission (MedPac) and the public by March 1st of every year the estimated conversion factor applicable for physician services for the following year and supply the underlying data for these estimates. So for 2009, the conversion factor estimate of 36.0666 was set on March 1, 2008.

Each of these factors is translated into a "relative value unit" and multiplied by a dollar amount supplied by CMS (Centers for Medicare and Medicaid Services). Payments are adjusted for geographical differences. Okay, that reads a little like a doctoral thesis on boredom in the 21st Century.
Let's describe it another way and see if it makes easier reading and more sense. Close to 8000 procedure codes are defined in the CPT® codebook. The AMA and CMS work together to analyze these codes from the perspective of the physicians providing the services. They take into account how much physician work, technical skill, physical and mental effort, judgment, stress, and potential risk is involved in each procedure. Consideration is also given to the expense involved in setting up and managing various types of physician practices and the costs of professional liability insurance in different geographic areas.

Several informational websites provide details about RBRVS. AMA and CMS in particular can provide you with additional reading material and background information on physician reimbursement.

Based on the factors listed above, each code is assigned a relative value unit. When a claim is received from the provider, the relative value unit for each CPT code is multiplied by the current CMS multiplier and a reimbursement is calculated for each service.

Suppose the CMS multiplier is $38. Reimbursement is calculated by multiplying the CMS conversion factor by the relative value assigned to the CPT® (or HCPCS) code.

In a case where the patient had two physician procedures/services performed, one with a relative value of 3 and one with a relative value of 6. The reimbursement would be:

CMS conversion factor	Relative Value	Total Reimbursement
38	X 3	= $114
38	X 6	= $228
		= $342

Sample RBRVS Reimbursement Chart:

CPT CODE	DESCRIPTION	RVU	CMS CONVERSION FACTOR	CMS REIMBURSEMENT
99213	Exam	1.02	X 38.0870	$38.84
38745	Axillary, lymphandectomy, complete	21.52	X 38.0870	$819.63
92997	Percutaneous transluminal artery balloon angioplasty, single vessel	17.31	X 38.0870	$659.29

Are you starting to see the importance of correct, complete medical coding to the healthcare reimbursement process? A breakdown anywhere along the chain of the healthcare documentation process can result in less than full reimbursement for provided services and can directly impact the financial wellbeing of a healthcare provider.

Also, notice RBRVS fits the fee-for-service and retrospective payment system categories because reimbursement is based on services provided to the patient. The reimbursement amounts are determined after the patient receives care and the claim is submitted.

I. **MULTIPLE CHOICE.**
   Choose the best answer.

   1. The primary entity using the RBRVS reimbursement methodology is _____.
      - ○ the military
      - ○ the teachers' union
      - ● Medicare
      - ○ all of the above

   2. What type of code is used to determine the relative value unit?
      - ○ ICD-9-CM diagnosis code
      - ● CPT code
      - ○ ICD-9-CM procedure code
      - ○ none of the above

   3. The reimbursement amount for the RBRVS system is based on the relative value unit and the _____.
      - ● CMS multiplier
      - ○ patient's geographical location
      - ○ type of specialty used
      - ○ age of the patient

   4. The RBRVS reimbursement system sets reimbursement rates for physician services based on which of the following factors?
      - ○ practice expense
      - ○ professional liability
      - ○ physician work
      - ● all of the above

   5. The RBRVS reimbursement system is an example of what type of reimbursement methodology?
      - ● fee-for-service
      - ○ episode-of-care

Managed Care

Reimbursement based on:
Services provided to the patient

1. Self-pay
2. Retrospective payment
☑ 3. **Managed care**

As you learned earlier, in recent decades third-party and government payers have evolved from being the ones who paid the bills to taking an active part in influencing patient healthcare decisions and provider reimbursement.

Managed care can operate under a fee-for-service model or under an episode-of-care model. Managed care simply means the third-party payer takes an active role in influencing cost and quality through its policies and provisions.

A simple example of a managed care policy is pre-authorization. The third-party payer requires the patient to obtain approval from the insurance company prior to scheduling surgery as a condition for the third-party payer to reimburse the provider for the surgery claim. If the patient fails to get prior approval, the third-party payer may pay a significantly reduced amount or not pay at all. Pre-authorization allows the insurance company (third-party payer) to influence the patient's decision-making by requiring second opinions or conservative therapy first. The insurance company can review healthcare documentation prior to the surgery and educate providers and patients about length of stay limitations and so forth.

Managed care may operate under a fee-for-service model or an episode-of-care model. Let's take a look at a few fee-for-service managed care payment methodologies.

I. **MULTIPLE CHOICE.**
   Choose the best answer.

   1. Managed care means the third-party payer takes an (●active, ○inactive) role in influencing cost and quality.

   2. The requirement for the patient to obtain approval from the insurance company prior to scheduling a procedure is known as (●pre-authorization, ○managed care)

   3. Pre-authorization allows (○the patient, ●the third-party payer) to make decisions requiring second opinions or conservative therapy prior to surgery.

Health Maintenance Organizations (HMOs)

Are you tired of the repetition yet? Hope not—because here it comes again! The primary factor in fee-for-service is that reimbursement is based on services provided to the patient. If a managed care payer is determining reimbursement on services provided, then it fits the fee-for-service category.

Although we haven't included managed care directly under the retrospective payment system category, fee-for-service HMOs and PPOs do use a retrospective payment model.

HMOs, or health maintenance organizations, exercise the most control over patient choice and provider treatment options. HMOs follow a set of care guidelines patients must follow in order to receive maximum benefits. A structure common to many HMOs is the requirement for a patient to choose a primary care physician. The primary care physician acts as a gateway to all medical services. The patient must obtain a referral by the primary care physician in order to see a specialist or authorize other types of treatment. Another structure seen in HMOs is case management. Patients with certain illnesses—cancer, diabetes, asthma—are assigned a case manager who coordinates patient care to reduce overlapping care, duplication of treatments, and so forth.

HMOs (third-party payers) contract with physicians, physician groups, hospitals, and clinics to provide care under the terms of the HMO. HMO patients are seen at steeply discounted rates and providers have a "pipeline" of patients through the HMO.

Under the fee-for-service HMO model, both the patient and the provider must follow the care guidelines set by the HMO in order to receive maximum reimbursement.

> We've placed a visual aid in the appendix on page 171.

The patient and provider receive the maximum contracted benefit when they follow the HMO guidelines.

> We've placed a visual aid in the appendix on page 172.

The patient and provider do not receive the maximum benefit (in this case a reduction of $35) when they do not follow the plan guidelines of the managed-care payer (HMO). The difference may or may not be billed to the patient based on the plan provision/provider policy.

I. **TRUE/FALSE.**
   Mark the following true or false.

   1. Many HMOs require a patient to choose a primary care physician.
      - ● true
      - ○ false

   2. Fee-for-service HMO's use a self-payment model.
      - ○ true
      - ● false

   3. HMOs contract with healthcare providers to provide care at discounted rates.
      - ● true
      - ○ false

Preferred Provider Organizations (PPOs)

Preferred provider organizations are a less restrictive type of managed care. Third-party payers contract with healthcare providers for discounted rates. If a covered patient elects to see a preferred provider in the preferred provider "network," the patient pays a smaller amount than if the patient elects to see a provider outside of the preferred provider network.

Highlights

Preferred providers are providers who have contracted with third-party payers to provide services at a discounted rate for insurance plan members.

> We've placed a visual aid in the appendix on page 173.

The patient visits a provider who is contracted with Sun Valley Group to provide services at a discounted rate (preferred provider rate).

> We've placed a visual aid in the appendix on page 174.

The patient has the option to visit a physician who is not contracted to provide discounted services for Sun Valley Group participants. The patient has the option but the patient pays more for the services of the out-of-network provider.

Fee-For-Service Summary

Of course, this list of fee-for-service models is not exhaustive. In addition to those covered, a number of other fee-for-service models exist, including point-of-service plans, exclusive-provider-organizations, private policy (indemnity), and many others.

All fee-for-service reimbursement methodologies have a few common elements:

- Fee-for-service providers are reimbursed for each service they provide.
- The more services a fee-for-service provider renders, the more reimbursement the provider receives.
- Most fee-for-service reimbursement methodologies are based on a retrospective payment system. Reimbursement amounts are determined after the patient has already received the services.
- Discounted fee-for-service arrangements are common.
- The difference between the amount billed by the provider and the amount paid by a third-party payer in a fee-for-service environment may or may not be billed to the patient. Contractual agreements between patient, provider, and third-party payer determine whether or not the patient is billed some or all of the difference.
- Medicare pays physicians using the resource-based relative value system, a discounted fee-for-service system.
- Some states use the resource-based-relative-value-system multiplied by some form of a conversion factor for their Medicaid reimbursement, while others use a state mandated Medicaid fee schedule or a combination of both.

Reimbursement based on:
Services provided to the patient

1. Self-pay
2. Retrospective payment
    a. fee schedules
    b. usual, customary, and reasonable
    c. RBRVS (resource-based relative value scale)

3. Managed care
    a. HMOs
    b. PPOs

Review: Managed Care

I. **TRUE/FALSE.**
   Mark the following true or false.

   1. HMOs exercise control over patient choice and provider treatment options.
      - ● true
      - ○ false

   2. Members of an HMO may be required to obtain pre-authorization prior to scheduling surgery.
      - ● true
      - ○ false

   3. Patients that belong to an HMO may be required to obtain a referral from their primary care physician in order to see a specialist.
      - ● true
      - ○ false

   4. In HMOs the patients pay a smaller amount if they see physicians out of the "network."
      - ○ true
      - ● false

   5. Managed care organizations operate only under the fee-for-service model.
      - ○ true
      - ● false

Episode-of-Care

We'll leave fee-for-service and turn our attention to episode-of-care reimbursement methods.

Episode-of-care reimbursement models don't pay based on individual services rendered. Episode-of-care models determine payment based on the "unit of time" a patient was treated for a certain thing (e.g. surgery, long-term treatments). A unit of time may be a visit (encounter for care) or a daily, monthly, or other specified time period of care.

In the next several lessons, we'll take a closer look at some major types of episode-of-care reimbursement methodologies: managed care, global and prospective payment systems.

Since we most recently discussed managed care, let's start with the managed care episode-of-care reimbursement method.

> **Highlights**
>
> In the physician-based system, episode-of-care models determine payment based on the "unit of time" a patient is treated.

Managed Care – Capitation

Reimbursement based on:
Patient's condition/illness
A specified time period

☑ 1. Managed Care – Capitation
2. Global payment/Prospective payment
3. Prospective payment

Capitation is a reimbursement method used by some managed care plans. The third-party payer contracts with the healthcare provider(s) to pay a flat fee per individual enrolled in the healthcare plan. The actual services provided to the patient—few or numerous—don't affect the reimbursement to the provider.

Happy Health Wellness HMO, Inc. has contracted with Derek Shepherd, M.D., to be a participating primary care physician in their network. The contract, in part, states the following method of reimbursement: Dr. Derek Shepherd shall be reimbursed on a per-member per-month (PMPM) basis. Dr. Shepherd shall receive a check on the first of each month based on the number of patients who have signed up with him for care. The payment methodology is broken down as follows:

- *Age 0–1year: $17.88/PMPM–vaccinations will be paid separately*
- *Age 2–4yrs: $17.88/PMPM–vaccinations will be paid separately*
- *Age 5–12yrs: $11.54/PMPM*
- *Age 13–20 yrs: $9.82/PMPM*
- *Age 21–49 yrs: $ 8.94/PMPM*
- *Age 50–60 yrs: $10.72/PMPM*
- *Age 61–64yrs: $11.53/PMPM*

Additionally, Dr. Shepherd may collect the copays from the patient as determined by the patient's policy.

A phrase commonly heard in the industry to refer to capitation payments is PMPM or "per member per month." The provider receives a set amount "per member per month." If the rate is $17—the provider receives $17/PMPM.

Under capitation reimbursement, the provider is paid the same rate for a patient with complex medical needs who is seen frequently as for a healthy patient who rarely seeks treatment. Capitation allows for certainty for the third–party payer and the provider because rates are set. The third-party payer knows what the cost will be for each member. The provider knows they are responsible for providing care for a given number of patients and will have a set income for those patients. However, the provider absorbs a certain degree of risk because how many patients will need high levels of care in a given month is unknown. Providers need a high enough capitation rate to balance those risks and average a positive cash flow.

Capitation Chart

Month	# of Patients Enrolled	Capitation Rate	Capitation Reimbursement	Actual Cost
January	212	$12	$2544	$2300
February	233	$12	$2796	$2990
March	210	$12	$2520	$1860
April	194	$12	$2328	$2410
May	260	$12	$3120	$2207
June	251	$12	$3012	$2825
Average	227	$12	$2720	$2432

This simplified example shows an average cost over six months to treat the average of 227 patients of $2432. The provider is reimbursed the same amount per patient regardless of the cost of treatment: $12. The provider had an average profit margin of $288 per month for treating patients under this managed care capitation agreement.

I. **TRUE/FALSE.**
   Mark the following true or false.

   1. The abbreviation PMPM in reference to capitation payments means per member per month.
      - ● true
      - ○ false

   2. Under the capitation reimbursement method the number of services provided to the patient affects the reimbursement to the provider.
      - ○ true
      - ● false

   3. Capitation does not provide any risk of financial loss to the provider since the same rate is paid for each patient.
      - ○ true
      - ● false

   4. The episode-of-care reimbursement methodology determines payment based on the patient's condition, disease or unit of time.
      - ● true
      - ○ false

   5. The capitation reimbursement method is the best method of reimbursement for physicians whose patients have complex medical needs.
      - ○ true
      - ● false

Global Payment/Prospective Payment Systems

Reimbursement based on:
Patient's condition/illness
A specified time period

1. Managed Care – Capitation
☑ 2. Global payment/Prospective payment
3. Prospective payment

Global payment. Sounds like it covers pretty much everything; *global* is certainly an all-inclusive word! Global reimbursement is a fixed amount of money or a lump-sum payment designated to cover a related group of services by multiple providers.

Global payments usually go hand in hand with prospective payments, so let's define prospective payment as well.

> ### Prospective: The act of looking forward
> When the costs of healthcare services are projected and allowable reimbursement amounts set for future healthcare services, this is called a **prospective payment system.**

Third-party payers have set up a number of prospective global payment systems, particularly government third-party payers.

An example of a **global prospective payment system** is the Medicare system used to reimburse home health services: HHPPS, or home health prospective payment system. Medicare pays for speech therapy, physical therapy, occupational therapy, nursing visits, home health aide visits, and other related home health costs with one payment to the Home Health Agency. The agency then distributes payment to all the professionals and agencies providing home health services.

Consider a patient receiving home healthcare services following a stroke:

Annette receives a daily home health aide visit and twice-weekly physical and occupational therapy to assist her with grooming, dressing, and transfer skills. She has no speech difficulty so she does not receive any occupational therapy for speech. A skilled nurse comes in daily for the first two weeks, then twice weekly, and finally bi-weekly as Annette progresses and is able to prepare her own medication. She also receives oxygen and oxygen supplies from a local supplier.

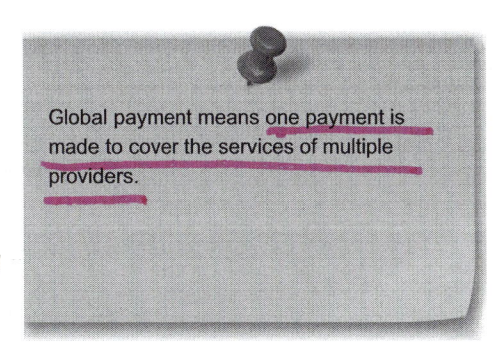

> Global payment means one payment is made to cover the services of multiple providers.

Although Annette receives services from a physical therapist, occupational therapist, skilled nurse, medical supply company, and a nurses' aide, the third-party payer will send one payment to the Home Health Agency for 60 days of care. The lump-sum payment will be distributed to the other professionals by the Home Health Agency.

HHPPS is a global payment system.

I. FILL IN THE BLANK.
Enter the correct word in the blank provided.

1. A _prospective payment system_ is when allowable reimbursement amounts are set for future healthcare services.

2. _Global reimbursement_ is a fixed amount of money designated to cover a related group of services by more than one provider.

3. An example of the global prospective payment system is the _Medicare System_ used to reimburse home health services.

Home Health Prospective Payment System (HHPPS)

HHPPS is also a prospective payment system because Medicare does not receive the bill and "tally up" each individual service to determine the payment amount. HHPPS sets reimbursement rates in advance for home health care. The HHPPS system uses a multiplier, known as HHRG (home health resource group), and operates by setting a fixed rate for home health services based on historical data. Once this fixed rate is set, adjustments may be made for severely acute patients or for patients receiving care in more (or less) expensive geographic areas.

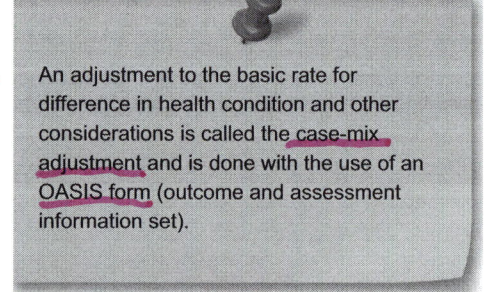

> An adjustment to the basic rate for difference in health condition and other considerations is called the case-mix adjustment and is done with the use of an OASIS form (outcome and assessment information set).

The fact that reimbursement rates are set for future services and are paid for 60-day blocks of time means the HHPPS is a prospective payment system and not a retrospective payment system.

The CMS website describes the HHPPS global payment system as follows:

Medicare pays home health agencies (HHAs) a predetermined base payment. The payment is adjusted for the health condition and care needs of the beneficiary. The payment is also adjusted for the geographic differences in wages for HHAs across the country. The adjustment for the health condition, or clinical characteristics, and service needs of the beneficiary is referred to as the case-mix adjustment. The home health PPS will provide HHAs with payments for each 60-day episode of care for each beneficiary. If a beneficiary is still eligible for care after the end of the first episode, a second episode can begin; there are no limits to the number of episodes a beneficiary who remains eligible for the home health benefit can receive. www.cms.hhs.gov/HomeHealthPPS

Government sets reimbursement rate based on historical data for home health care costs.

⬇

Patient receives home health care services coordinated by a home health agency.

⬇

Documentation is coded.

⬇

Home health agent completes a patient assessment (called an OASIS) to adjust for variables like critical care versus low–level rehabilitative care.

⬇

Claim is sent to Medicare/Medicaid.

⬇

Claim is reimbursed in one lump sum using OASIS*, predetermined based payment amount (HHRG).

⬇

Check is sent to home health agency and dispersed to professionals and providers who provided home health services.

---

*Outcome and Assessment Information Set is the assessment tool used to adjust for differences in health conditions, geographic differences etc.

HHPPS is both a global payment system and a prospective payment system.

Review: Payment/Prospective Payment Systems

I. **TRUE/FALSE.**
   Mark the following true or false.

   1. The home health prospective payment system is an example of a global prospective payment system.
      - ● true
      - ○ false

   2. HHPPS, a prospective payment system, projects the cost of home healthcare services and sets the allowable reimbursement amounts for future home healthcare services.
      - ● true
      - ○ false

   3. Under the HHPPS system, each provider receives a separate payment for the services provided.
      - ○ true
      - ● false

   4. Global reimbursement is a fixed payment amount designated to cover a related group of services by multiple providers.
      - ● true
      - ○ false

   5. Reimbursement rates under the HHPPS are paid for 30-day blocks of time.
      - ○ true
      - ● false

Prospective Payment Systems

Reimbursement based on:
Patient's condition/illness
A specified time period

1. Managed Care – Capitation
2. Global payment/Prospective payment
☑ 3. Prospective payment

Under a prospective payment system, the third-party payer is interested in looking at averages over time and paying the average cost for each patient instead of the actual cost for each patient. Prospective payment systems establish payment amounts in advance for future healthcare services.

Highlights

Not all prospective payment systems are global payment systems. Global payment means multiple providers share a single payment. Prospective payment systems can be set up so that different payments are made to different providers—although the payment amount is not based on what was actually done but on historical averages.

The HHPPS system is a prospective payment systems based on a unit of time (60 days) with adjustments for healthcare considerations. However, prospective payment systems may be based on time units or based on services for specific conditions or diseases.

Another example of a time unit-based reimbursement system is the Indian Health Services reimbursement system. IHS sets a per-diem (daily) rate. Reimbursement rates are set based on historical daily costs of providing healthcare services and then reimbursed on a per-day basis or per-encounter basis.

Government Prospective Payment Systems

Government Prospective Payment Systems

You've walked through one prospective payment system in some detail—HHPPS. Let's look at some of the other prospective payment systems in common use and walk through a few more examples.

Provider	System	Calculation Unit
Home Health Agencies	HHPS - Home Health Prospective Payment System	HRG w/case-mix adjustment
Ambulatory Surgical Centers	ASCPPS - Ambulatory Surgical Center Prospective Payment System	ASC (Ambulatory Surgical Center) Group
Skilled Nursing Facilities (Nursing Homes)	SNFPPS - Skilled Nursing Facility Prospective Payment System	RUG - Resource Utilization Group
Outpatient Hospital Services	OPPS - Outpatient Prospective Payment Systems	APC - Ambulatory Payment Classification
Inpatient Hospital Services	IPPS - Inpatient Prospective Payment System	DRG - Diagnosis-related Groups

HHPPS is a prospective payment system based on a unit of time. Let's take a look at a prospective payment system based on disease or condition. First, review in your mind the basics of prospective payment systems:

- Payment is not made on individual services provided but on allowable rates.
- Allowable rates are based on historical information/data and set for future healthcare costs.
- Procedures performed must be related to the reported diagnosis.
- Prospective payment systems are based on averages and projections, not on actual services provided to individual patients.

Outpatient Prospective Payment System

Hospitals provide both inpatient and outpatient services. Outpatient services are reimbursed by Medicare and Medicaid through a prospective payment system known as the outpatient prospective payment system. (Not too creatively named!)

Services listed in the CPT® procedure coding book and the HCPCS book are analyzed by CMS (Centers for Medicaid and Medicare Services). CMS looks at what resources are required to provide the services. Clinical services that require similar resources are grouped into payment classifications called Ambulatory Payment Classifications.

Reimbursement rates are set for each Ambulatory Payment Classification and reimbursement is based on the Ambulatory Payment Classifications listed on the patient's claim. Keep in mind the claim also lists the patient's diagnosis (ICD codes), and the procedures performed must "make sense" for the diagnosis listed.

CMS sets reimbursement rates for each APC (ambulatory payment classification).

⬇

Patient receives outpatient services at a hospital.

⬇

Documentation is coded.

⬇

Codes are transferred to claim.

⬇

Claim sent to third-party payer.

⬇

CPT and HCPCS codes are grouped to the appropriate APC (Ambulatory Payment Classification) by third-party payer.

⬇

Claim is reimbursed based on pre-set APC rates.

*Notes: Hospitals may be paid for more than one APC per encounter.
Adjustments may be calculated for geographic area.

I. MATCHING.
Match the following steps to the number which represents the order in which they happen.

1. _d_ 1
2. _a_ 2
3. _f_ 3
4. _c_ 4
5. _g_ 5
6. _b_ 6
7. _e_ 7

A. Patient receives outpatient services at a hospital.
B. CPT and HCPCS codes are grouped to the appropriate APC (Ambulatory Payment Classification) by third-party payer.
C. Codes are transferred to claim.
D. CMS sets reimbursement rates for each APC (ambulatory payment classification).
E. Claim is reimbursed based on pre-set APC rates.
F. Documentation is coded.
G. Claim sent to third-party payer.

OPPS Example

On March 20, 2007, Tony Soprano was brought to New Jersey South General Hospital's E.R. for a gunshot wound to the upper right arm and left upper chest. Dr. Tony Gates examined Mr. Soprano and ordered x-rays of the right upper arm and a 2-view chest x-ray to determine the amount of damage. Dr. Gates performed an exploration of a penetrating wound to the chest and right upper arm and was able to remove two bullets. He also performed a complex wound closure—8 cm to the chest and 8 cm to the right arm. Mr. Soprano was given an arm strap to support the arm.

Listed below are the codes and charges:

APC CODES	CPT® CODES	DESCRIPTION	CHARGES	REIMBURSEMENT
0023	20101	Exploration of penetrating wound chest	$800.00	$609.68
0023	20103-51-RT	Exploration of penetrating wound of right arm	$750.00	$304.84
0135	13121-51-RT	Complex wound repair right arm 7.5 cm	$350.00	$149.10
0135	13122-RT	Complex wound repair right arm add'l .5 cm	$300.00	$149.10
0135	13101-51	Complex wound repair of chest 7.5 cm	$400.00	$149.10
0135	13101	Complex wound repair chest, add'l .5cm	$350.00	$149.10
0614	G0382	Medicare's emergency room level 3 exam	$175.00	$138.32
0058	29240-51-RT	Strapping for right shoulder	$100.00	$48.90
0260	71010	X-ray of chest, 2 view	$100.00	$46.23

0260	73090-RT	X-ray of right upper arm, 2-view	$125.00	$46.23
TOTALS			CHARGES $3,450.00	REIMBURSEMENT $1,790.60

CPT codes are grouped into APC classifications. Notice, for example, two different x-rays with two different CPT codes (71010 and 73090-RT) are both grouped into APC classification 0260 (Level I plain film except teeth).

A reimbursement rate is set for APC classification 0260 (Level I plain film except teeth) of $46.23 by CMS, and all x-rays in this classification are reimbursed at the same level. Did you notice the billed charges were different for each x-ray?

APC payment rates are maximum reimbursement rates. For surgical claims, only the highest APC (highest dollar value) is paid at the maximum rate; all other surgical charges are paid at 50% of the maximum rate. X-rays/radiology are not considered surgical procedures, so they are paid at the maximum rate.

Excerpt from 2008 APC Group List, published by CMS:

APC	Group Title	Relative Weight*	Payment Rate
0023	Exploration penetrating wound	9.5721	609.68
0135	Level III skin repair	4.6816	298.19
0614	Level III emergency visit	2.1716	138.32
0058	Level I strapping and cast application	1.1272	71.79
0260	Level I plain film except teeth	0.7259	46.23

*Relative weights are assigned based on complexity of procedure, cost to provide procedure, degree of skill required, and other factors.

Medical coding specialists do not need to understand every nuance of relative weight payment. However, medical coding specialists do need to understand the general principles involved in outpatient prospective payment systems. Accurate medical coding, accurate medical billing, accurate auditing, and accurate reimbursement all depend on the teamwork of medical coders, medical billers, healthcare auditors, and the reimbursement specialists they work with.

CMS Descriptions

The Centers for Medicaid and Medicare describes the Outpatient Prospective Payment Systems for outpatient hospital services (APC) and outpatient surgical center services (ASC) as follows:

Ambulatory payment classification (APC) system – A coding and reimbursement hierarchy for outpatient services that organizes CPT® and HCPCS codes into several hundred groups. These service bundles are the basis for Medicare reimbursement for many outpatient hospital services. Some hospital services such as anesthesia, recovery room, and many drugs and supplies are considered bundled into the APC payment and, therefore, reimbursement is minimized.

Ambulatory Surgical Center – The ASC payment system replaces the current procedure classification and payment system with a new system that links ASC facility payments to Medicare payments to hospital outpatient departments for the same procedure. CMS uses the ambulatory payment classifications (APCs) established in the hospital OPPS as the mechanism for grouping ASC procedures. The APC relative payment weights for hospitals become the basis for calculating ASC payment rates under the new payment system.

Episode-of-Care
Reimbursement based on:
Patient's condition/illness
A specified time period

1. Managed Care – Capitation
    a. Capitation HMO

2. Global payment/Prospective payment
    a. HHPPS

3. Prospective payment
    a. IHS
    b. OPPS
    c. ASC
    d. APC
    e. SNF PP
    f. IPPS

Prospective Payment Systems

Medicare, Medicaid, Blue Cross, TRICARE, and many other third-party payers use a prospective payment system to reimburse for inpatient healthcare. Hospital inpatient visits vary from the routine to the most extended, complex cases. The inpatient prospective payment system (IPPS) looks at the historical costs for providing inpatient services for a given diagnosis and sets a payment amount for treatment of the diagnosis in patients fitting a certain profile (age, sex, complications, etc).

In 1983, Medicare used the historical information to introduce an inpatient prospective payment system based on DRGs (diagnosis related groups). Diagnosis related groups list over 500 diagnoses and the "cluster" of procedures, treatments, and supplies hospitals used to treat those diagnoses for patients fitting a specific profile (age, sex, weight, complications, etc.)

When the inpatient facility submits a claim to a third-party payer, the claim is "torn down" and then categorized into a diagnosis related group. The diagnosis related group determines the amount the hospital will receive.

CMS sets DRGs (diagnosis related groups) for classifying hospital services for a given diagnosis.

⬇

Patient receives inpatient services at a hospital.

⬇

Documentation is coded.

⬇

Codes are transferred to claim.

⬇

Claim sent to third-party payer.

⬇

Third-party payers assign itemized charges to appropriate DRG classification based on diagnosis and patient profile.

⬇

Claim is reimbursed at DRG rate.*

DRG reimbursement may be adjusted for special factors such as hospitals serving high indigent population, teaching facilities, etc.

Steps in Determining a PPS Payment

Step 1 - Hospitals submit a bill for each Medicare patient they treat to their Medicare fiscal intermediary (a private insurance company that contracts with Medicare to carry out the operational functions of the Medicare program). Based on the information provided on the bill, the case is categorized into a diagnosis related group (DRG), which determines how much payment the hospital receives.

Step 2 - The base payment rate is comprised of a standardized amount, which is divided into a labor-related and nonlabor share. The labor-related share is adjusted by the wage index applicable to the area where the hospital is located and if the hospital is located in Alaska or Hawaii, the nonlabor share is adjusted by a cost of living adjustment factor. This base payment rate is multiplied by the DRG relative weight.

Step 3 - If the hospital is recognized as serving a disproportionate share of low-income patients, it receives a percentage add-on for each case paid through the PPS. This percentage varies depending on several factors, including the percentage of low-income patients served. It is applied to the DRG-adjusted base payment rate, plus any outlier payments received.

Step 4 - If the hospital is an approved teaching hospital it receives a percentage add-on payment for each case paid through the PPS. This percentage varies depending on the ratio of residents-to-beds.

Step 5 - Next, the costs incurred by the hospital for the case are evaluated to determine whether it is eligible for additional payments as an outlier case. This additional payment is designed to protect the hospital from large financial losses due to unusually expensive cases. Any outlier payment due is added onto the DRG-adjusted base payment rate.

Severity-Adjusted DRGs

In 2008, a new element, known as severity-adjusted DRG was added to provide additional payment for patients with extremely high acuity (the sickest patients).

Today, many hospital billing systems include automatic DRG calculations to help the medical coder and medical biller determine the ordering of diagnosis and procedure codes to maximize reimbursement.

DRG Example

Patient Frank Stein, age 23, is hospitalized for 4 days following a motorcycle versus automobile accident. Total charges for the 4-day hospital stay are $8,800.

The itemized bill is analyzed and the diagnosis/services fit DRG 32 (Concussion Age > 17 without complications or comorbidities). After adjustments, the hospital reimburses $4022.

The hospital billed the third-party payer $8800 for Frank's stay and received $4022 based on the DRG reimbursement.

Review: Prospective Payment System

I. **TRUE/FALSE.**
   Mark the following true or false.

   1. All third-party payers use the outpatient prospective payment system as the basis for reimbursement.
      ○ true
      ○ false

   2. Discounted fee-for-service arrangements are common in prospective payment systems.
      ○ true
      ○ false

3. Reimbursement under the outpatient prospective payment system is based on Ambulatory Payment Classifications.
   ○ true
   ○ false

4. All prospective payment systems are considered global payment systems.
   ○ true
   ○ false

5. The ambulatory surgical center payment system uses the ambulatory payment classifications as the mechanism for grouping ASC procedures.
   ○ true
   ○ false

Concluding Thoughts

Medical coding and billing specialists work hard to create an accurate claim. Accuracy is important not only to assure proper payment for each individual patient, but also because encoded medical records (and, subsequently, healthcare claims) are the raw data used to track trends and determine future reimbursement rates.

As a medical coder, you will work with elements of prospective and retrospective payment systems. Depending on your work environment, you may find yourself working with software that automatically assigns APCs or revenue codes or other billing elements when you input the ICD-9, CPT®, or HCPCS codes. You might be working with a system that doesn't do any of that for you. The claims reviewers may request additional information from you to justify your code choices.

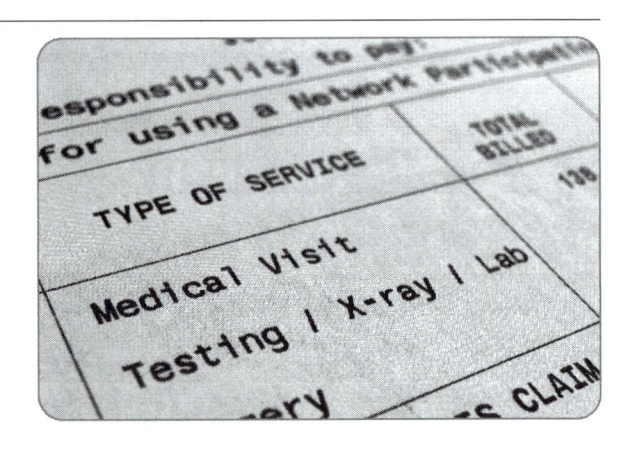

The Healthcare Reimbursement module isn't designed to teach you every detail of preparing or calculating reimbursements. The objective is for you to understand the basic reimbursement systems and the important ways all of the pieces of documentation, coding, billing, and reimbursement interconnect.

Unit 7
Quality Assurance Practices and Regulatory Compliance

Quality Assurance Practices and Regulatory Compliance – Introduction

The efforts of companies, corporations, and public agencies to comply with and verify compliance with laws and regulations pertinent to operating within an industry(ies) is regulatory compliance. Regulatory compliance is achieved by setting up processes and systems such as training personnel, implementing QA processes, auditing, or designating departments and/or individuals to direct compliance efforts.

We are now going to deal with issues of quality assurance and regulatory compliance. Way, way back, many modules ago (isn't it amazing to think you've come so far that you can say that!), you learned healthcare is a highly regulated industry because of four important factors:

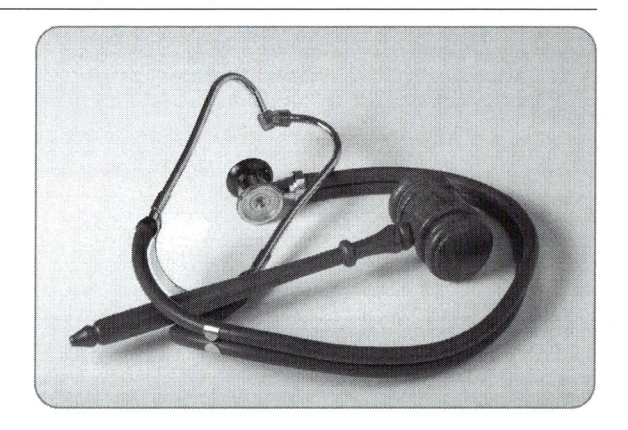

1. Healthcare involves quality of life and death issues.
2. Healthcare is expensive.
3. People and companies want to be protected from fraud and abuse.
4. Government subsidizes billions of dollars for healthcare.

Regulatory compliance is a **big** deal in healthcare. *Healthcare personnel are expected to know and apply the relevant rules and regulations in the treatment of patients, in the documentation of healthcare, and in healthcare billing.* The government takes seriously issues of fraud and abuse.

Regulatory Agencies

We are now going to bring together many concepts you were introduced to here and there throughout your training program. In the Healthcare Structure and Organization module, you first read about the Department of Health and Human Services. The Department of Health and Human Services is tasked with governing and regulating healthcare in the United States.

The Centers for Medicare and Medicaid develop many of the rules and regulations for the healthcare industry, but the Office of Inspector General (OIG) is tasked with "protect(ing) the integrity of DHHS programs…through a nationwide network of audits, investigations, inspections, and other mission-related functions."

When the Office of Inspector General finds issues of fraud, abuse, or illegal activity, the complaints are directed to the Department of Justice (DOJ) for criminal prosecution. The DOJ is an independent law enforcement agency and is not under the DHHS umbrella.

DHHS
Department of Health and Human Services
Parent agency governing and regulating healthcare.

CMS
Centers for Medicaid/Medicare
Develops rules and regulations.

OIG
Office of Inspector General
Monitors for compliance and turns suspected fraud and abuse over to the DOJ.

DOJ
Department of Justice
Prosecutes fraud and abuse.

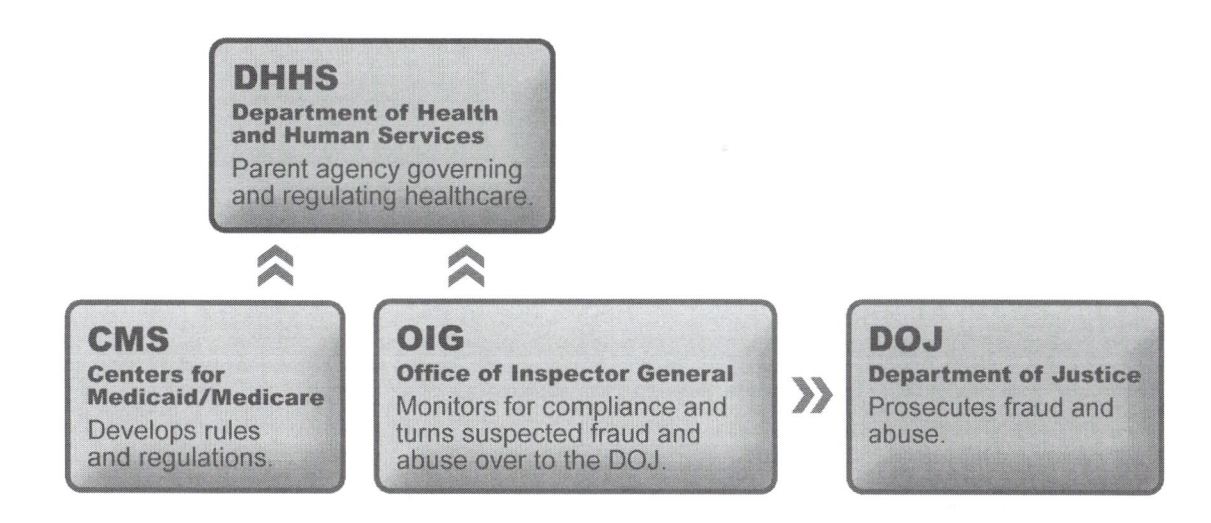

Although some healthcare providers are dishonest and engage in fraudulent practices, it is the goal of the vast majority of healthcare providers to understand and achieve regulatory compliance through education and adoption of quality assurance practices.

Audits

The tool used by regulatory agencies and healthcare providers to educate, check for regulatory compliance, and update policies and procedures is an audit.

An **audit** is a review of the steps in the healthcare documentation process. Audits may be conducted while the patient is actively receiving healthcare (concurrently) or once the patient is no longer actively receiving care, when the documentation/billing process is complete or substantially complete (retrospectively).

Healthcare documentation audits look at some or all of the following:

- The patient's medical record
- Copies of the charge slip(s) or superbill(s) for the specified date(s) of service
- Diagnosis, procedural, and supply code assignments
- Claims sent to patient and third-party payer
- EOBs/remittance advice received from third-party payers to verify payment posting and rejection management

Audits may reveal several things and can be of great importance to a medical facility. HIM (health information management) audits may uncover:

- Lack of documentation in the medical record to support charges and fees
- Undercoding
- Upcoding
- Unbundling
- Not coding to the highest specificity
- Diagnoses not properly matched to procedure codes
- Duplicate billing
- Lost or missing charge slips or visits not billed or coded

> **Highlights**
>
> **Audits**: review of the steps in the healthcare documentation process.
>
> **Concurrent review**: review done while the patient is actively receiving care.
>
> **Retrospective review**: review done after the patient has received care.

When one or more of these issues are identified, a plan or procedure can be implemented to correct past problems and prevent future problems.

When an audit is performed by personnel within a healthcare provider organization, it is called an internal audit. When an audit is performed by personnel or agencies outside of the healthcare provider organization, it is called an external audit. External audits may be conducted at the request of the healthcare provider or at the request of an outside party or agency.

I. MULTIPLE CHOICE.
Choose the best answer.

1. A review done while a patient is actively receiving care is called a(n) _____.
   - ○ retrospective review
   - ● concurrent review
   - ○ audit
   - ○ check up

2. A review of the steps in the healthcare documentation process is called a(n) _____.
   - ○ retrospective review
   - ○ concurrent review
   - ● audit
   - ○ external audit

3. A review done after the patient has received care is called a(n) _____.
   - ● retrospective review
   - ○ concurrent review
   - ○ audit
   - ○ internal audit

4. An audit performed by personnel within a healthcare organization is called a(n) _____.
   - ○ retrospective review
   - ○ concurrent review
   - ● internal audit
   - ○ external audit

Internal Audits

Internal audits are performed by personnel within the healthcare provider organization. The Office of the Inspector General (OIG) recommends all healthcare providers institute an ongoing regulatory compliance program that includes an ongoing internal auditing program. The OIG offers compliance guidance and compliance resource material to assist healthcare providers in setting up and maintaining a regulatory compliance program.

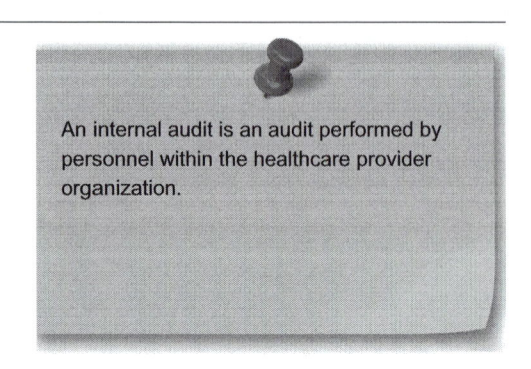

An internal audit is an audit performed by personnel within the healthcare provider organization.

The OIG offers a 7-step basic guide for individual and small group practices to create and maintain a voluntary regulatory compliance program:

1. Conduct internal monitoring and auditing through the performance of periodic audits.
2. Implement compliance and practice standards through the development of written standards and procedures.
3. Designate a compliance officer or contact(s) to monitor compliance efforts and to enforce practice standards.
4. Conduct appropriate training and education on practice standards and procedures.
5. Respond appropriately to detected violations through the investigation of allegations and the disclosure of incidents to appropriate government entities.
6. Develop open lines of communication, such as discussions at staff meetings, regarding how to avoid erroneous or fraudulent conduct to keep employees updated regarding compliance activities.
7. Enforce disciplinary standards through well-publicized guidelines.

The OIG also offers compliance plans for hospitals as well as several other provider types. These can be found by going to http://www.oig.hhs.gov and selecting Fraud Prevention & Detection.

Healthcare providers range in size from a single physician working out of a small office to a group of radiology physicians providing contracted services to entire outpatient departments within large inpatient hospitals.

Every healthcare provider, large or small, should have an ongoing internal auditing program in place to monitor regulatory compliance. Whether the provider is a single physician office operating with a single staff member or a large outpatient facility, staff should include internal review and auditing as part of an ongoing healthcare documentation integrity and regulatory compliance program.

> **Highlights**
>
> The key to a successful internal auditing program for regulatory compliance is ensuring that the facility or provider makes changes when problems or issues are discovered.

The key to a successful internal auditing program for regulatory compliance is ensuring that the facility or provider makes changes when problems or issues are discovered.

Sample Coding Auditor Job Description

The Coding Audit and Education Specialist is responsible for auditing/analyzing the coding/documentation for accuracy and completeness of coded medical records. This person works closely with the staff in education and auditing functions as it pertains to coding. This person will also assist the supervisor with QA on each provider and with audits requested by other departments. The person in this position works independently under the supervision of the Coding Supervisor. Work situations require extensive knowledge, experience, and training in coding and medical terminology, and the ability to effectively teach others. A high degree of diplomacy, tact, and excellent customer service and communications skills are required.

I. **TRUE/FALSE.**
   Mark the following true or false.

   1. Healthcare institutions do not have a need for internal audits except when potential problems arise.
      - ○ true
      - ● false

   2. The OIG recommends that all healthcare providers institute an ongoing regulatory compliance program, including an internal auditing program.
      - ● true
      - ○ false

   3. Smaller healthcare operations have little need for internal audits-- only large operations need to worry about them.
      - ○ true
      - ● false

   4. Facilities or providers should make changes when problems or issues are discovered in an internal audit.
      - ● true
      - ○ false

Reasons for Audits

The purpose of internal audits is to proactively address non-compliance issues and to work to bring the healthcare provider into compliance and keep the healthcare provider in compliance.

Let's look at some potential problems that might be uncovered during an audit:

- missed charges
- not properly matching diagnoses with procedures or services
- unbundling services that are usually billed under one code
- inadequate documentation in the medical record
- illegible documentation in the medical record
- documentation that is spread out and not centralized for easy review in the medical record
- upcoding to gain higher reimbursement
- unnecessary medical services
- undercoding for services that require higher level of service codes
- billing for postoperative services during the global surgery period when there should be no charge
- not billing for services provided in the global period that are not related to the surgery for which the patient is currently in the postoperative period
- locating errors on the charge slip or superbill (old codes, deleted codes, etc.)

Highlights

Undercoding: Selecting codes at a lower level than the service documented

Upcoding: Selecting codes at a higher level than the service documented

Unbundling: Billing two or three procedures when the services are typically covered by a single comprehensive code

- failure to write off insurance discounts
- duplicate billing

If an audit uncovered a duplicate billing, the first step would be to correct the duplicate billing. However, correcting the duplicate billing would be just a first step. Next, the audit should lead the provider to find out how the duplicate billing occurred. Was it a one-time error? Is there a software problem? Is the biller adequately trained? Once answers to these questions are found, education, training, new policies, processes, procedures, or other appropriate measures can be taken to reduce the chances of future duplicate billing errors occurring.

Internal audits help the facility to achieve and maintain regulatory compliance.

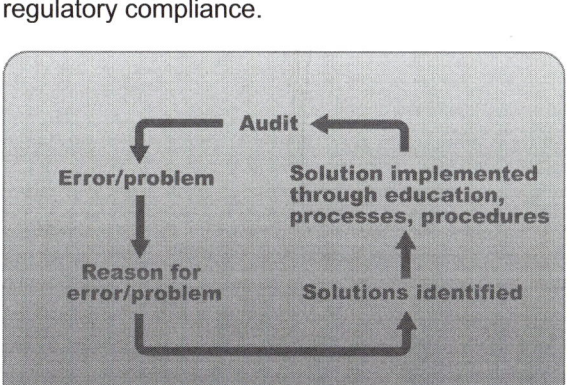

Auditing is an ongoing process to assure quality care and avoid non-compliance.

I. TERMINOLOGY.
Enter each term in the space provided. Read the definition and description for each term.

1. **Undercoding** _____

   Selecting codes at a lower level than the service documented.

2. **Upcoding** _____

   Selecting codes at a higher level than the service documented.

3. **Unbundling** _____

   Billing two or three procedures when the services are typically covered by a single comprehensive code.

Sample Coding and Billing Audit Form

The Office of Inspector General offers many tools for performing internal audits. Review the samples: Coding and Billing Audit, Documentation Audit, and Medicare/Medicaid Complaint and Resolution Form.

> We've placed a visual aid in the appendix on page 175.

> We've placed a visual aid in the appendix on page 176.

> We've placed a visual aid in the appendix on page 177.

Review: Audits

I. **MATCHING.**
   Match the correct term to the definition.

1. _D_ A provider requests the coding specialist to review documentation in patients' medical records, superbills, verify diagnosis codes, support procedure code assignments, and review third-party payer EOBs.

2. _A_ This regulatory agency governs and regulates healthcare in the United States.

3. _B_ Claims filed with the knowledge of falsity on the claim.

4. _E_ When fraudulent claims are discovered during an external audit, these are turned over to this government organization for investigation.

5. _C_ This regulatory agency protects the integrity of the Department of Human and Health Services through audits and investigations.

A. DHHS
B. fraudulent claims
C. OIG
D. internal audit
E. DOJ

External Audits

Government has an interest in making sure facilities are compliant; they have a financial stake and a mandated legal responsibility to monitor compliance. Several other players in the healthcare industry also have a vested interest in monitoring healthcare providers' healthcare documentation practices. Third-party payers, such as insurance companies, have financial interests in the healthcare documentation process. Employers are concerned that their employees are receiving quality services. Workers' compensation patients want to be sure that their documentation accurately reflects their medical condition when their case is reviewed.

> When an audit is performed by a regulatory agency or by an independent auditor outside of the healthcare provider organization (at the request of the healthcare provider or at the request of an individual, company, or agency outside of the healthcare provider), it is an external audit.

External audits of the healthcare documentation process may be conducted at the request of the provider or at the request of an outside individual, company or agency. External audits are conducted by individuals outside of the healthcare provider organization.

External audits fall under two categories: reactive and proactive.

Proactive External Audits

If the terms *proactive* and *reactive* have a familiar feel, the mists of memory from the Healthcare Structure and Organization module are floating around in your mind. You first learned about proactive and reactive audits back there.

A proactive audit is a routine or random audit to check the healthcare provider's compliance with rules and regulations for:

- providing services
- documenting healthcare services
- billing healthcare services

> **Highlights**
>
> The Joint Commission: An independent, not-for-profit organization, The Joint Commission accredits and certifies more than 15,000 health care organizations and programs in the United States. Joint Commission accreditation and certification is recognized nationwide as a symbol of quality that reflects an organization's commitment to meeting certain performance standards.

The auditing team(s) would meet with various departments or individuals to review healthcare practices—including coding and billing practices—by reviewing healthcare records, codes, and bills (claims).

Auditors would identify deficiencies and the provider would submit a corrective plan of action to address the deficiencies. In most cases, the audit team would work with the facility team to assist in addressing issues and implementing better practices and procedures.

Proactive audits may be conducted by an accounting firm, an independent consulting firm, third-party payers (on the records for their insured only), or the facility may choose to participate in a voluntary third-party audit program, such as the Joint Commission.

If routine issues are uncovered and are appropriately addressed, healthcare providers can benefit from a proactive external audit. If, however, an external proactive audit uncovers a pattern of noncompliance, grossly inadequate healthcare documentation practices, or suspected fraud or abuse, the findings will be turned over to an investigating agency.

I. **FILL IN THE BLANK.**
   Enter the correct word in the blank provided.

   1. Auditors identify _____ and the provider submits a corrective plan of action to address them.

   2. A proactive audit is a _____ audit to check the healthcare provider's compliance with rules and regulations.

3. Facilities may choose to participate in a voluntary third-party audit program such as the

   _____.

4. If issues are uncovered and appropriately addressed, healthcare providers can benefit from a

   _____.

Medical Humor

You know you're a real auditor when:

You keep a calibration certificate for the thermometer.

You issue nonconformities to everyone including hotels, airlines, restaurants, rental car agencies, your paperboy, etc. whether you are auditing them or not.

You say, "How do you know that? Do you have any objective evidence to support that?" when all that someone said was, "Gee, isn't it a nice day?"

You can read any and all documents upside down and right to left.

Reactive External Audits

External audits conducted as the result of a complaint, concern, or suspicion of wrongdoing are reactive external audits.

Reactive audits may be prompted by any one of a number of things: an individual patient complaint, a pattern of unusual billing activity reported by one or more third-party payers, or a complaint by another healthcare provider.

The audit may be restricted to the specific circumstances that prompted the audit or the audit may be expanded to a full-scale healthcare audit. Government regulatory agencies, third-party payers, and others with contractual relationships with the healthcare provider may conduct reactive audits.

If evidence of deliberate wrongdoing/fraudulent activity is found, the information will be turned over to an investigating agency for review (most commonly the Department of Justice).

Highlights

Erroneous claim: Claim filed with innocent errors on them due to faulty processes, misinterpretation, or other negligence.

Fraudulent claim: Claim filed with knowledge of falsity of the claim.

The Department of Justice has made fighting fraud and abuse in the healthcare industry one of the Department's top priorities. Healthcare fraud and abuse drains billions of dollars from Medicare and Medicaid, which provide essential healthcare services to millions of elderly, low income, and disabled Americans. The impact of healthcare fraud and abuse cannot be measured in terms of dollars alone. While healthcare fraud burdens our nation with enormous financial costs, it also threatens the quality of healthcare.*

(*Department of Justice. www.usdoj.gov/dag/pubdoc/health98.htm)

If a healthcare provider is found to be making fraudulent claims instead of simply erroneous claims, legal action may be pursued against those participating in the fraud.

In many cases, reactive external audits find no evidence of deliberate wrongdoing and serve to help the healthcare facility address deficiencies in their healthcare documentation practices.

> The Department [of Justice] continues to prevent fraud and abuse in a number of ways: by encouraging providers to police their own activities through compliance programs; and by sponsoring consumer outreach initiatives, such as the consumer's fraud hotlines, to involve patients with first-hand knowledge in the detection of fraudulent practices. Settlement agreements with providers also emphasize future prevention efforts.*
>
> (*Department of Justice. www.usdoj.gov/dag/pubdoc/health98.htm)

Highlights

Qualitative analysis: Review that deals with accuracy—is the information contained in the record correct?

Quantitative analysis: Review that deals with completeness—is the record thorough and complete?

Medical coding specialists occupy a central role in the healthcare documentation process. Often it is the medical coding specialist who first becomes aware of problems with insufficient, incomplete, or inaccurate documentation.

Even if a medical coding specialist is not directly assigned the role of "auditor," the medical coder has a responsibility to look for acceptable documentation through ongoing qualitative and quantitative analysis of the medical record.

I. FILL IN THE BLANK.
Enter the correct word in the blank provided.

1. A review that deals with accuracy is called a _____.

2. A claim filed with knowledge of falsity of the claim is called a _____.

3. Reactive external audits are the result of _____ concern, or suspicion of wrongdoing.

4. A review that deals with completeness is called a _____.

5. A claim filed with innocent errors due to faulty processes, misinterpretation, or other negligence is called an _____.

RAC: The Recovery Audit Contractor

Every year, Medicare receives over 1.2 billion claims. This is equivalent to 9,579 claims received per minute! With so many claims, improper payments are bound to happen. In 2006, Medicare began a three-year demonstration project with contracted auditors in several states across the country to find out more about the situation. During that time period, it was discovered that there had been $371.5 million in improper payments! 96% of those were overpayments, and only 4% were underpayments.

These payment errors included some of the following:

- Incorrect payment amounts
- Non-covered services
- Incorrectly coded services
- Duplicate services/claims

The Recovery Audit Contractor program (RAC), as it is called, is now being implemented all around the country. Centers for Medicare and Medicaid Services (CMS) has contracted several auditing companies to be their eyes and ears, performing audits to determine these improper payments. As you head into the workforce, you will no doubt hear more about these new audits.

Conclusion and Review

Medical coding specialists have a responsibility to understand and adhere to the coding guidelines outlined in the ICD-9-CM codebook, the CPT® codebook and the HCPCS codebook. Medical coders have a responsibility to know the guidelines and, to the best of their ability, apply the guidelines correctly and thoroughly.

Keeping up to date on coding changes and updates, actively participating in quality assurance programs designed to assure regulatory compliance, and maintaining quality healthcare services to all patients should be your focus as part of the healthcare support services team.

I. **TRUE/FALSE.**
   Mark the following true or false.

   1. A proactive external audit is typically performed by either an independent consulting firm or by the staff in the provider's office.
      - ○ true
      - ○ false

   2. If evidence of deliberate fraudulent billing is found during an audit process, this information is turned over by the OIG to the DOJ for further investigation.
      - ○ true
      - ○ false

   3. The Office of Inspector General offers tools to perform internal audits.
      - ○ true
      - ○ false

   4. A reactive audit is performed after a complaint has been filed or a third-party payer suspects fraudulent billing.
      - ○ true
      - ○ false

   5. Coding specialists are very busy with their day-to-day jobs so if they do not keep up with the rules and regulations, the Office of the Inspector General will overlook this during an audit.
      - ○ true
      - ○ false

Unit 8
Diagnostic Related Groups

Diagnostic Related Groups – Introduction

It is important as an inpatient medical coder for you to learn how the selection of the correct diagnoses and procedures relate to the proper reimbursement of the services rendered at a hospital. Accurate coding leads to the correct reimbursement for the hospital. Likewise, inaccurate coding leads to incorrect reimbursement, including hospitals receiving a lower or higher reimbursement than they are entitled to for the services provided. It is the coder's responsibility to make sure that all code assignments are as accurate as they can possibly be.

> **Example:**
>
> A medical record is reviewed and the codes are submitted for reimbursement. The coder missed reporting a complication or comorbidity diagnosis, which would have resulted in a higher weighted Diagnostic Related Group.

The example above demonstrates the most common way hospitals receive a lower reimbursement than they are entitled to. When a coder doesn't report all of the diagnoses documented by the physician, this can cause lost revenue for the hospital. Ultimately, this is the responsibility of the medical coder.

All hospitals want to receive the maximum amount of reimbursement they are entitled to. After all, they have to run a business. However, at same time they are concerned with making sure no fraudulent coding is being performed at their facility. As we discussed in the Documentation, Confidentiality, and Ethics module, coders have a professional and an ethical standard to uphold. Not only are the hospitals responsible for internally auditing the accuracy of their codes, but government agencies are also concerned with making sure the healthcare coding and billing process is fair and accurate.

> **Example:**
>
> A medical coder reports a diagnosis that was not documented by the physician, which resulted in reporting a higher weighted Diagnostic Related Group.

In this example, the diagnosis reported resulted in the hospital receiving more reimbursement than they were entitled to. Whether this diagnosis was reported intentionally to receive a higher reimbursement or not, the hospital would have pay back the amount they were improperly reimbursed.

Fortunately, the process for coding inpatient hospital encounters is very specific and thorough. If you stick to the process and the codebooks, you will have no worries about coding accuracy. This unit will present information that will help you understand the structure and purpose of the inpatient reimbursement system, which is called the Inpatient Prospective Payment System (IPPS).

The factor that determines whether or not the hospital receives the correct reimbursement is the proper assignment of the **diagnostic related group** (DRG). In this module you will learn what a DRG is and what factors influence how DRGs are assigned.

What Is A DRG?

(handwritten: for inpatient hospital services)

Diagnosis Related Groups (which we will hereafter refer to as DRGs—I know, I know, not another medical acronym!) were created with a simple intent: create a system of classification that can put all Medicare patients receiving hospital care into groups and assign the groups reimbursement values. The system was begun in the 1980s and, like the ICD classification system, has undergone many changes and upgrades over the years.

Today, the DRG classifications system is used by Tricare, Medicaid, Blue Cross, Medicare and others to simplify the reimbursement process. Hospital inpatient services will fall into one of the over 500 DRG classifications, which were created using figures and data from past patients and procedures. The prospective payment system utilizes this data to calculate a single cost for the various hospital services provided to patients. This makes the reimbursement process (in theory) more streamlined and economical.

In this unit, we will look at how hospital inpatients are placed into the proper groups. The first question we must answer is *what information is used to place an inpatient in a particular DRG?*

There are five factors that influence the assignment of DRGs:

1. Principal and secondary diagnosis and procedure codes
2. Sex
3. Age
4. Discharge status
5. Presence or absence of complications and comorbidities (CCs)

(handwritten: 5 factors)

It is essential you understand how each of these factors influences the assignment of DRGs.

DRG Assignment Factors

We said earlier that there are five factors that influence the assignment of DRGs:

1. Principal and secondary diagnosis and procedure codes
2. Sex
3. Age
4. Discharge status
5. Presence or absence of complications and comorbidities (CCs)

There are a couple of ways that the correct Diagnosis Related Group can be determined. You can use a DRG book and manually look up the DRG codes based on the information in the medical record (like you do for diagnosis and procedure codes). You can also utilize coding software to find the correct DRG code. In the interest of time (and to save you from having to labor through another huge book), we will be using coding software to determine DRGs. In the practicum portion of this program (that's the next module), we will teach you how to use your software to find the correct DRG. For now, we want to look at the factors that influence the DRG assignment. At this point, we will go through each of these factors individually to illustrate how pulling details from the medical reports will determine the proper DRG.

125

Principal and secondary diagnosis and procedure codes

The principal and secondary diagnosis codes are the starting point for the selection of the correct DRG. As a medical coder, if you are able to identify all the principal and secondary diagnosis and procedure codes, this will lead to the assignment of the correct DRG the majority of the time.

DRG Assignment – Sex

There are specific DRGs that are gender specific. Certain diagnoses and procedures can only be assigned to males or females. Example of these include the following:

Male Diagnosis Examples:
- prostate cancer
- hydrocele
- torsion of testicle

Male Procedure Examples:
- orchiectomy
- prostatectomy
- vasectomy

Female Diagnosis Examples:
- endometriosis of ovary
- dysmenorrhea
- tubal pregnancy

Female Procedure Examples:
- salpingo-oophorectomy
- hysterectomy
- dilation and curettage (D&C)

The following are examples of DRGs which can only be assigned to male patients.

DRG 350 Inflammation of the Male Reproductive System

DRG351 Sterilization, Male

The following are examples of DRGs which can only be assigned to female patients.

DRG 353 Pelvic Evisceration, Radical Hysterectomy and Radical Vulvectomy

DRG 356 Female Reproductive System Reconstructive Procedures

DRG Assignment – Age

If a patient in one age group tends to use more resources than patients in another age group, then the DRGs are split according to age.

The following are examples of DRGs which can only be assigned to specific age groups:

DRG 070 Otitis Media and URI, Age 0-17

DRG 294 Diabetes, Age Greater than 35

DRG Assignment – Discharge Status

When a patient is transferred from one acute care hospital to another or from one acute care hospital to a certain postacute care provider (ex. skilled nursing facility), the payment for some DRGs is reduced.

The following are examples of DRGs in which the reimbursement is affected by the discharge status of the patient.

DRG 014 Intracranial Hemorrhage or Cerebral Infarction

DRG 121 Circulatory Disorders with Acute Myocardial Infarction and Major Complications, Discharged Alive

DRG Assignment – Presence or Absence of Complications and Comorbidities (CCs)

The presence of a complication or comorbidity diagnosis can cause the patient's case to be grouped into the higher-weighted DRG.

The following are examples of DRGs in which the reimbursement is affected by the presence or absence of complications and comorbidities.

DRG 452 Complications of Treatment with CC

DRG 453 Complications of Treatment without CC

I. **TRUE/FALSE.**
   Mark the following true or false.

   1. DRGs are used only by Medicare.
      ○ true
      ⊗ false

   2. If you know the primary diagnosis code, you do not need any other information to find the DRG.
      ○ true
      ⊗ false

   3. *DRG* stands for Diagnosis Related Group.
      ⊗ true
      ○ false

   4. DRGs allow for differences in costs of resources used.
      ⊗ true
      ○ false

   5. You have to use the "Numeric Index to Procedures" to locate a DRG.
      ○ true
      ⊗ false

DRG Relative Weight

Each DRG is assigned a **relative weight**. This weight reflects the resource consumption associated with the patient's hospital stay. As discussed at the beginning of this module, the higher the relative weight, the greater the reimbursement to the hospital. The amount the hospital is reimbursed is based on which DRG is assigned so it is imperative you assign the correct DRG.

To determine the amount the hospital is reimbursed for any DRG, you would **multiply the national average payment by the relative weight**. The National Average Payment Table is supplied in books and software.

> **Example:**
>
> A patient was diagnosed with viral meningitis and was assigned the DRG 076 Viral Meningitis without CC/MCC.

In this example, the reimbursement can be calculated for this DRG by locate the national average payment amount in a published table. The amount listed is $4,402.00. Now locate the relative weight for this DRG. The weight listed is 0.8595. The reimbursement for this DRG would be calculated as follows:

National Average Payment	$4,402.00
Relative Weight	X 0.8595
	$3,783.51

The hospital would receive reimbursement in the amount of $3,783.51 for this patient. When a patient is assigned the incorrect DRG this can result in the hospital receiving a lower or higher reimbursement than they are entitled to. In the example above the patient was diagnosed with viral meningitis so the patient was assigned to DRG 076. However, if the patient was incorrectly assigned to DRG 075, the following reimbursement would be paid to the hospital:

National Average Payment	$8,573.39
Relative Weight	X 1.6730
	$14,343.28

In comparing the reimbursement amounts for these two DRGs the difference is $10,559.77. Therefore, the hospital would be reimbursed $10,559.77 more than they were entitled to for a patient who was incorrectly assigned to DRG 075. Small errors can add up to big payment mistakes.

Terminology – Lesson 1

The following are some common terms related to the assignment of DRGs.

I. **TERMINOLOGY.**
   Enter each term in the space provided. Read the definition and description for each term.

   1. **against medical advice** _____

   Discharge status of patients who leave the hospital without notifying hospital personnel.

   2. **arithmetic mean length of stay** _____

   Also referred to as AMLOS, this is the average number of days patients within a given DRG stay in the hospital. Also referred to as the average length of stay.

   3. **base rate** _____

   Number assigned to a hospital used to calculate DRG reimbursement. This rate varies from hospital to hospital.

   4. **case-mix index** _____

   Also referred to as CMI, this is the sum of all DRG relative weights, divided by the number of Medicare cases.

   5. **CC** _____

   Complication or comorbid condition.

II. **MATCHING.**
    Match the correct term to the definition.

    1. _B_ case-mix index
    2. _D_ against medical advice
    3. _E_ CC
    4. _A_ Arithmetic mean length of stay
    5. _C_ base rate

    A. Referred to as the average length of stay.
    B. The sum of all the DRG relative weights divided by the number of Medicare cases.
    C. Number used to calculate DRG reimbursement for each hospital.
    D. Status of the patient who leaves the hospital without the knowledge of hospital personnel.
    E. Complication or comorbidity.

III. **FILL IN THE BLANK.**
     Enter the correct word in the blank provided.

     1. The _arithmetic mean_ length of stay for the DRG 386 is 17.9 days.

     2. Number which varies from hospital to hospital used to calculate DRG reimbursement is called the _Base rate_.

     | base rate |
     | against medical advice |
     | arithmetic mean |
     | comorbidity |
     | case-mix index |

3. A patient who left the hospital without the knowledge of the attending physician would be assigned a discharge status of _against medical advice_

4. A complication is a condition which occurs after the patient is admitted and _comorbidity_ is a condition which is present upon admission.

5. To find the _case mix index_ for each month you would calculate the sum of all the DRG weights for each month and divide it by the number of Medicare cases for each month.

Terminology – Lesson 2

The following are some common terms related to the assignment of DRGs.

I. TERMINOLOGY.
Enter each term in the space provided. Read the definition and description for each term.

1. **charges** _____

The dollar amount of hospital bills.

2. **comorbidity** _____

Pre-existing condition which, because of its presence with a specific diagnosis, causes an increase in length of stay by at least one day in approximately 75% of the cases.

3. **complication** _____

Condition that arises during the hospital stay which prolongs the length of stay by at least one day in approximately 75% of the cases.

4. **diagnosis-related group** _____

Also referred to as a DRG, this is one of the valid classification of diseases in which patients demonstrate similar resource consumption and length-of-stay patterns.

5. **discharge** _____

When the patient leaves an acute care hospital after completion of treatment.

II. MATCHING.
Match the correct term to the definition.

1. __D__ comorbidity
2. __B__ charges
3. __A__ discharge
4. __E__ complication
5. __C__ diagnosis-related group

A. Completion of treatment at an acute care hospital.
B. The amount of the hospital bill.
C. Classification of diseases with similar length of stay patterns.
D. Pre-existing condition which causes an increase in the patient's hospital length-of-stay.
E. Condition which occurs after admission to the hospital and prolongs the patient's hospital length-of stay.

III. FILL IN THE BLANK.
Enter the correct word in the blank provided.

1. A __diagnosis-related group__ is used to classify diagnosis and procedures with similar resource consumption patterns.

2. The patient underwent surgery and developed a __complication__ of intraoperative bleeding.

3. After discharge from the hospital the patient was given a summary of the __charges__ for the hospital stay.

4. Upon completion of treatment for the patient's principal diagnosis the physician decided to __discharge__ the patient.

5. The patient was admitted with a principal diagnosis of congestive heart failure and a secondary diagnosis of atrial fibrillation. This secondary condition is called a __comorbidity__.

diagnosis-related group
charges
discharge
complication
comorbidity

Terminology – Lesson 3

The following are some common terms related to the assignment of DRGs.

I. TERMINOLOGY.
Enter each term in the space provided. Read the definition and description for each term.

1. **discharge status** _____

   Disposition of the patient at discharge (for example: left against medical advice, discharged home, transferred to an acute care hospital, expired).

2. **grouper** _____

   The software program that assigns DRGs.

3. **major diagnostic category** _____

   Also known as MDC, this is a broad classification of diagnoses typically grouped by body system.

4. **nonoperating room procedure** _____

   Procedure which does not require the use of the operating room and that can affect DRG assignment.

5. **operating room procedure** _____

   Procedure that falls into a group of procedures which require the use of an operating room.

II. MATCHING.
Match the correct term to the definition.

1. _B_ grouper
2. _C_ operating room procedure
3. _E_ major diagnostic category
4. _D_ discharge status
5. _A_ nonoperating room procedure

A. Does not require the use an operating room.
B. Program which assigns DRGs.
C. Type of procedure which requires the use of an operating room.
D. Location the patient is discharged.
E. Classification of diagnoses grouped by body system.

III. **FILL IN THE BLANK.**
   Enter the correct word in the blank provided.

   1. The _discharge status_ of the patient was left against medical advice.

   2. A minor procedure performed in the patient's hospital room is considered a _nonoperating room_ procedure.

   3. The program which a medical coder uses to assign DRGs is called a _grouper_.

   4. A _major diagnostic category_ is the grouping of diagnoses by body system.

   5. A procedure which requires the patient to be placed under general anesthesia is called an _operating room_ procedure.

grouper
nonoperating room
operating room
discharge status
major diagnostic category

Terminology – Lesson 4

The following are some common terms related to the assignment of DRGs.

I. **TERMINOLOGY.**
   Enter each term in the space provided. Read the definition and description for each term.

   1. **other diagnosis** _____

   Conditions which exist at the time of admission or develop subsequently that affect the treatment received and/or the length of stay.

   2. **outliers** _____

   Cases in which the costs for treating the patient are extraordinarily high in relation to the costs for other patients in the same DRG.

   3. **per diem rate** _____

   Payment made to the hospital from which a patient is transferred for each day of stay.

   4. **PMDC** _____

   This is also referred to as pre-MDC. There are 9 DRGs to which cases are directly assigned based upon procedure codes. Cases are assigned to these DRGs before classification to an MDC. The PMDC includes DRGs for heart, liver, bone marrow, simultaneous pancreas/kidney transplant, pancreas transplant, lung transplant, and three DRGs for tracheostomies.

   5. **principal diagnosis** _____

   Condition established after study to be chiefly responsible for occasioning the admission of the patient to the hospital for care.

II. MATCHING.
Match the correct term to the definition.

1. **E** principal diagnosis
2. **B** outliers
3. **A** per diem rate
4. **D** PMDC
5. **C** other diagnosis

A. Amount the transferring hospital receives.
B. Cases where the cost for patient's in the same DRG are high.
C. Conditions which affect the treatment of the patient.
D. Cases directly assigned to this classification based upon specific procedure codes.
E. The condition responsible for the patient's admission to the hospital.

III. FILL IN THE BLANK.
Enter the correct word in the blank provided.

1. A patient was transferred to another hospital for continued treatment so the transferring hospital received a **per diem rate** for the services provided to this patient.
2. The patient was admitted for treatment of a fracture and the patient is also a diabetic. The condition of diabetes would be reported as a(n) **other diagnosis**.
3. An example of a procedure which would be assigned to a(n) **pre-MCC** is a kidney transplant.
4. The cost of a patient's hospital stay was higher than usually for the DRG which was assigned to the patient so this would be considered an **outlier**.
5. A patient was admitted for chest pain which the physician determined was due to pneumonia so this is the patient's **principal diagnosis**.

other diagnosis
outlier
per diem rate
principal diagnosis
pre-MDC

Terminology – Lesson 5

The following are some common terms related to the assignment of DRGs.

I. TERMINOLOGY.
Enter each term in the space provided. Read the definition and description for each term.

1. **principal procedure** _____

Procedure performed for definitive treatment rather than diagnostic or exploratory purposes, or that was necessary to treat a complication. The principal procedure usually is related to the principal diagnosis.

2. **relative weight** _____

Also referred to as RW, this is the assigned weight that is used to reflect the resource consumption associated with each DRG. The higher the relative weight, the greater the reimbursement to the hospital.

3. **surgical hierarchy** _____

Ordering of surgical cases from the most to least resource intensive.

4. **transfer** _____

Situation in which the patient is transferred to another acute care hospital for related care.

5. **volume** _____

Number of patients in each DRG.

II. MATCHING.
Match the correct term to the definition.

1. _D_ transfer
2. _A_ relative weight
3. _C_ volume
4. _E_ principal procedure
5. _B_ surgical hierarchy

A. Reflects the resource consumption for each DRG.
B. Surgical cases ordered from most to least resource intensive.
C. Number of patients in each DRG.
D. Patient sent to another hospital for continued treatment.
E. Performed for definitive treatment.

III. FILL IN THE BLANK.
Enter the correct word in the blank provided.

1. The number of patient's assigned to each DRG is called the _volume_.

2. When surgical cases are ordered from the most to least resource intensive this is called the _surgery hierarchy_.

relative weight
volume
transfer
principal procedure
surgical hierarchy

3. The higher the _relative weight_ the greater the reimbursement the hospital receives.

4. It was necessary to _transfer_ this patient because of the complex nature of the patient's condition.

5. When several procedures are performed, the one most related to the principal diagnosis is assigned as the _principal procedure_.

Answer Key

Coding for Physician's Services

Coding at the Physician's Office

I. TRUE/FALSE.
1. true
2. false
3. false

Physician Care at Outside Facilities

I. TRUE/FALSE.
1. true
2. true
3. false

Review: Coding for Physicians

I. TRUE/FALSE.
1. false
2. true
3. true
4. false
5. true

Review: Coding for Facilities

I. TRUE/FALSE.
1. true
2. false
3. false
4. true
5. true

Chargemaster/Fee Schedule

I. MULTIPLE CHOICE.
1. all of the above
2. fee schedule
3. vary from provider to provider
4. every year (at a minimum)

Review: Outpatient Billing Process

I. TRUE/FALSE.
1. false
2. false
3. true
4. true
5. false

Life Cycle of a Claim

The Four Steps in a Medical Claim

I. TRUE/FALSE.
1. false
2. false
3. true
4. true
5. false

Claim Submission – 3rd-Party Payer Information

I. TRUE/FALSE.
1. false
2. true
3. false
4. false
5. true

Claim Forms

I. MULTIPLE CHOICE.
1. UB-04
2. CMS-1500
3. UB-04
4. CMS-1500

Claims Processing

I. MULTIPLE CHOICE.
1. electronically
2. CMS-1500
3. all of the above
4. the healthcare provider and the third-party payer
5. pre-edit claims for errors

Claims Adjudication

I. MATCHING.
1. C. the process of reviewing a claim and deciding what claims are to be paid
2. A. a percentage of medical bills the policyholder is responsible for after deductible is met
3. B. a company that handles, formats, screens, and distributes claims
4. E. an overview of claims recently filed on a patient
5. D. the sending of the claim by the healthcare provider to the third-party payer

Managing Claims

I. MULTIPLE CHOICE.
1. both A and B
2. an aging report
3. the physician
4. all of the above
5. A remittance advice is sent to the healthcare provider.

139

Appealing Claims

I. TRUE/FALSE.
1. true
2. true
3. false
4. false
5. true

Completing the CMS-1500 Claim Form

Preparing Documentation

I. TRUE/FALSE.
1. true
2. false
3. false
4. true
5. true

Beginning Your CMS-1500: Items 1-3

I. MULTIPLE CHOICE.
1. 220 NORTH LAKE DRIVE
2. X
3. SMITH JONATHON A
4. all of the above
5. 08 10 1996

Patient and Insured information: Items 4-9

I. MATCHING.
1. A. patient
2. D. insured
3. B. secondary coverage
4. E. policyholder
5. C. primary coverage

Patient and Insured information: Items 10-13

I. TRUE/FALSE.
1. false
2. false
3. true
4. false
5. true

Beginning the Patient or Supplier Information: Items 14-18

I. MULTIPLE CHOICE.
1. the date of the injury
2. 02132009 02202009
3. dates the patient could not work
4. any healthcare provider seeking reimbursement
5. ALLEN A WILSON MD

Patient or Supplier Information: Item 24

I. MATCHING.
1. C. diagnosis pointer
2. E. NPI number
3. B. units of service
4. A. From _____ To _____ format
5. D. POS

Patient or Supplier Information: Items 25-33

I. TRUE/FALSE.
1. false
2. true
3. false
4. true
5. false

Completing the UB-04 Claim Form

Patient Information – Lesson 2

I. MULTIPLE CHOICE.
1. FL 3b will not change from one bill to the next
2. an outpatient encounter
3. 117 MARSH HARBOUR DR
4. 16
5. in the NUBC Official Data Specifications Manual

Patient Information – Exercise

I. TRUE/FALSE.
1. true
2. true
3. false
4. true
5. true
6. false
7. true
8. false
9. true
10. false

II. MATCHING.
1. H. Used to enter the patient date of birth
2. B. Used for referral source code
3. G. National Uniform Billing Committee
4. A. Form locator
5. J. Used to show the relationship of patient to the insured
6. D. The first adopted Uniform Bill
7. E. Used to enter the name of the patient
8. C. Used to code the priority of the encounter
9. F. Used by facilities to bill payers today
10. I. Electronic guide explaining how to complete the UB-04

Healthcare Provider Information – Lesson 2

I. MULTIPLE CHOICE.
1. only if the provider needs payments to be sent to an alternate address
2. assigned by the IRS
3. assigned by the third-party payer
4. no punctuation
5. is used for a number assigned by the National Plan and Provider Enumeration System

Healthcare Services Information – Lesson 1

I. TRUE/FALSE.
1. false
2. true
3. false
4. true
5. false

Reimbursement Methodologies

The Consumer

I. TRUE/FALSE.
1. false
2. false
3. true

Contract Relationships

I. TRUE/FALSE.
1. true
2. true
3. false

Payment

I. TRUE/FALSE.
1. false
2. true
3. true

Government

I. TRUE/FALSE.
1. true
2. false
3. true

Review: Healthcare Reimbursement

I. MULTIPLE CHOICE.
1. Government requires all payers to reimburse at the same rate for the same services.
2. government
3. managed-care coverage
4. patient ethnicity
5. lower premiums (rates)

Fee-For-Service and Episode-of-Care

I. TRUE/FALSE.
1. false
2. true
3. true

Self-Pay

I. FILL IN THE BLANK.
1. self-pay
2. third-party payer
3. Payment options

Retrospective Payment

I. FILL IN THE BLANK.
1. costs or charges
2. after
3. less than

Review: Fee-For-Service

I. MULTIPLE CHOICE.
1. fee-for-service
2. usual, customary, and reasonable
3. patient's condition or illness
4. retrospective
5. episode-of-care

Resource-Based Relative Value Scale (RBRVS)

I. MULTIPLE CHOICE.
1. Medicare
2. CPT code
3. CMS multiplier
4. all of the above
5. fee-for-service

Managed Care

I. MULTIPLE CHOICE.
1. active
2. pre-authorization
3. the third-party payer

Health Maintenance Organizations (HMOs)

I. TRUE/FALSE.
1. true
2. false
3. true

Review: Managed Care

I. TRUE/FALSE.
1. true
2. true
3. true
4. false
5. false

Managed Care – Capitation

I. TRUE/FALSE.
1. true
2. false
3. false
4. true
5. false

Global Payment/Prospective Payment Systems

I. FILL IN THE BLANK.
1. prospective payment system
2. global reimbursement
3. Medicare system

Review: Payment/Prospective Payment Systems

I. TRUE/FALSE.
1. true
2. true
3. false
4. true
5. false

Outpatient Prospective Payment System

I. MATCHING.
1. D. CMS sets reimbursement rates for each APC (ambulatory payment classification).
2. A. Patient receives outpatient services at a hospital.
3. F. Documentation is coded.
4. C. Codes are transferred to claim.
5. G. Claim sent to third-party payer.
6. B. CPT and HCPCS codes are grouped to the appropriate APC (Ambulatory Payment Classification) by third-party payer.
7. E. Claim is reimbursed based on pre-set APC rates.

Review: Prospective Payment System

I. TRUE/FALSE.
1. false
2. false
3. true
4. false
5. true

Quality Assurance Practices and Regulatory Compliance

Audits

I. MULTIPLE CHOICE.
1. concurrent review
2. audit
3. retrospective review
4. internal audit

Internal Audits

I. TRUE/FALSE.
1. false
2. true
3. false
4. true

Review: Audits

I. MATCHING.
1. D. internal audit
2. A. DHHS
3. B. fraudulent claims
4. E. DOJ
5. C. OIG

Proactive External Audits

I. FILL IN THE BLANK.
1. deficiencies
2. routine or random
3. Joint Commission
4. proactive external audit

Reactive External Audits

I. FILL IN THE BLANK.
1. qualitative analysis
2. fraudulent claim
3. complaint
4. quantitative analysis
5. erroneous claim

Conclusion and Review

I. TRUE/FALSE.
1. false
2. true
3. true
4. true
5. false

Diagnostic Related Groups

DRG Assignment Factors

I. TRUE/FALSE.
1. false
2. false
3. true
4. true
5. false

Terminology – Lesson 1

II. MATCHING.
1. B. The sum of all the DRG relative weights divided by the number of Medicare cases.
2. D. Status of the patient who leaves the hospital without the knowledge of hospital personnel.
3. E. Complication or comorbidity.
4. A. Referred to as the average length of stay.
5. C. Number used to calculate DRG reimbursement for each hospital.

III. FILL IN THE BLANK.
1. arithmetic mean
2. base rate
3. against medical advice
4. comorbidity
5. case-mix index

Terminology – Lesson 2

II. MATCHING.
1. D. Pre-existing condition which causes an increase in the patient's hospital length-of-stay.
2. B. The amount of the hospital bill.
3. A. Completion of treatment at an acute care hospital.
4. E. Condition which occurs after admission to the hospital and prolongs the patient's hospital length-of stay.
5. C. Classification of diseases with similar length of stay patterns.

III. FILL IN THE BLANK.
1. diagnosis-related group
2. complication
3. charges
4. discharge
5. comorbidity

Terminology – Lesson 3

II. MATCHING.
1. B. Program which assigns DRGs.
2. C. Type of procedure which requires the use of an operating room.
3. E. Classification of diagnoses grouped by body system.
4. D. Location the patient is discharged.
5. A. Does not require the use an operating room.

III. FILL IN THE BLANK.
1. discharge status
2. nonoperating room
3. grouper
4. major diagnostic category
5. operating room

Terminology – Lesson 4

II. MATCHING.
1. E. The condition responsible for the patient's admission to the hospital.
2. B. Cases where the cost for patient's in the same DRG are high.
3. A. Amount the transferring hospital receives.
4. D. Cases directly assigned to this classification based upon specific procedure codes.
5. C. Conditions which affect the treatment of the patient.

III. FILL IN THE BLANK.
1. per diem rate
2. other diagnosis
3. pre-MDC
4. outlier
5. principal diagnosis

Terminology – Lesson 5

II. MATCHING.
1. D. Patient sent to another hospital for continued treatment.
2. A. Reflects the resource consumption for each DRG.
3. C. Number of patients in each DRG.
4. E. Performed for definitive treatment.
5. B. Surgical cases ordered from most to least resource intensive.

III. FILL IN THE BLANK.
1. volume
2. surgical hierarchy
3. relative weight
4. transfer
5. principal procedure

147

Appendix

1500

HEALTH INSURANCE CLAIM FORM

APPROVED BY NATIONAL UNIFORM CLAIM COMMITTEE 08/05

| PICA | | | | | | | | | PICA |

CARRIER

1. MEDICARE ☐ (Medicare #) MEDICAID ☐ (Medicaid #) TRICARE CHAMPUS ☐ (Sponsor's SSN) CHAMPVA ☐ (Member ID#) GROUP HEALTH PLAN ☐ (SSN or ID) FECA BLK LUNG ☐ (SSN) OTHER ☐ (ID) | 1a. INSURED'S I.D. NUMBER (For Program in Item 1)

2. PATIENT'S NAME (Last Name, First Name, Middle Initial) | 3. PATIENT'S BIRTH DATE MM | DD | YY   SEX M ☐ F ☐ | 4. INSURED'S NAME (Last Name, First Name, Middle Initial)

5. PATIENT'S ADDRESS (No., Street) | 6. PATIENT RELATIONSHIP TO INSURED Self ☐ Spouse ☐ Child ☐ Other ☐ | 7. INSURED'S ADDRESS (No., Street)

CITY | STATE | 8. PATIENT STATUS Single ☐ Married ☐ Other ☐ | CITY | STATE

ZIP CODE | TELEPHONE (Include Area Code) ( ) | Employed ☐ Full-Time Student ☐ Part-Time Student ☐ | ZIP CODE | TELEPHONE (Include Area Code) ( )

9. OTHER INSURED'S NAME (Last Name, First Name, Middle Initial) | 10. IS PATIENT'S CONDITION RELATED TO: | 11. INSURED'S POLICY GROUP OR FECA NUMBER

a. OTHER INSURED'S POLICY OR GROUP NUMBER | a. EMPLOYMENT? (Current or Previous) YES ☐ NO ☐ | a. INSURED'S DATE OF BIRTH MM | DD | YY   SEX M ☐ F ☐

b. OTHER INSURED'S DATE OF BIRTH MM | DD | YY   SEX M ☐ F ☐ | b. AUTO ACCIDENT? YES ☐ NO ☐   PLACE (State) | b. EMPLOYER'S NAME OR SCHOOL NAME

c. EMPLOYER'S NAME OR SCHOOL NAME | c. OTHER ACCIDENT? YES ☐ NO ☐ | c. INSURANCE PLAN NAME OR PROGRAM NAME

d. INSURANCE PLAN NAME OR PROGRAM NAME | 10d. RESERVED FOR LOCAL USE | d. IS THERE ANOTHER HEALTH BENEFIT PLAN? YES ☐ NO ☐ If yes, return to and complete item 9 a-d.

READ BACK OF FORM BEFORE COMPLETING & SIGNING THIS FORM.

12. PATIENT'S OR AUTHORIZED PERSON'S SIGNATURE I authorize the release of any medical or other information necessary to process this claim. I also request payment of government benefits either to myself or to the party who accepts assignment below.

SIGNED _____ DATE _____

13. INSURED'S OR AUTHORIZED PERSON'S SIGNATURE I authorize payment of medical benefits to the undersigned physician or supplier for services described below.

SIGNED _____

PATIENT AND INSURED INFORMATION

14. DATE OF CURRENT: MM | DD | YY ILLNESS (First symptom) OR INJURY (Accident) OR PREGNANCY(LMP) | 15. IF PATIENT HAS HAD SAME OR SIMILAR ILLNESS. GIVE FIRST DATE MM | DD | YY | 16. DATES PATIENT UNABLE TO WORK IN CURRENT OCCUPATION FROM MM | DD | YY TO MM | DD | YY

17. NAME OF REFERRING PROVIDER OR OTHER SOURCE | 17a. | 17b. NPI | 18. HOSPITALIZATION DATES RELATED TO CURRENT SERVICES FROM MM | DD | YY TO MM | DD | YY

19. RESERVED FOR LOCAL USE | 20. OUTSIDE LAB? YES ☐ NO ☐ $ CHARGES

21. DIAGNOSIS OR NATURE OF ILLNESS OR INJURY (Relate Items 1, 2, 3 or 4 to Item 24E by Line)

1. |_____._____| 3. |_____._____|
2. |_____._____| 4. |_____._____|

22. MEDICAID RESUBMISSION CODE _____ ORIGINAL REF. NO. _____

23. PRIOR AUTHORIZATION NUMBER

24. A. DATE(S) OF SERVICE From MM DD YY To MM DD YY	B. PLACE OF SERVICE	C. EMG	D. PROCEDURES, SERVICES, OR SUPPLIES (Explain Unusual Circumstances) CPT/HCPCS	MODIFIER	E. DIAGNOSIS POINTER	F. $ CHARGES	G. DAYS OR UNITS	H. EPSDT Family Plan	I. ID. QUAL.	J. RENDERING PROVIDER ID. #
1									NPI
2									NPI
3									NPI
4									NPI
5									NPI
6									NPI

25. FEDERAL TAX I.D. NUMBER   SSN ☐ EIN ☐ | 26. PATIENT'S ACCOUNT NO. | 27. ACCEPT ASSIGNMENT? (For govt. claims, see back) YES ☐ NO ☐ | 28. TOTAL CHARGE $ | 29. AMOUNT PAID $ | 30. BALANCE DUE $

31. SIGNATURE OF PHYSICIAN OR SUPPLIER INCLUDING DEGREES OR CREDENTIALS (I certify that the statements on the reverse apply to this bill and are made a part thereof.)

SIGNED _____ DATE _____

32. SERVICE FACILITY LOCATION INFORMATION

a. NPI   b.

33. BILLING PROVIDER INFO & PH # ( )

a. NPI   b.

PHYSICIAN OR SUPPLIER INFORMATION

NUCC Instruction Manual available at: www.nucc.org   APPROVED OMB-0938-0999 FORM CMS-1500 (08-05)

150

HEALTH INSURANCE CLAIM FORM

1500
APPROVED BY NATIONAL UNIFORM CLAIM COMMITTEE 08/05

CHAMPION INSURANCE
CLAIMS DEPARTMENT
1463 ELM DRIVE
LINCOLN TN 12345

1. Insurance Type	[X] GROUP HEALTH PLAN
1a. INSURED'S I.D. NUMBER	YTH8568477882
2. PATIENT'S NAME	PALIN BARBIE J
3. PATIENT'S BIRTH DATE / SEX	04 18 1972 / F
4. INSURED'S NAME	PALIN BARBIE J
5. PATIENT'S ADDRESS	13 MATTELL LN
CITY / STATE	MIDDLETON WI
ZIP CODE	53562
TELEPHONE	(842) 7790450
6. PATIENT RELATIONSHIP TO INSURED	[X] Self
7. INSURED'S ADDRESS	13 MATTELL LN
CITY / STATE	MIDDLETON WI
ZIP CODE	53562
TELEPHONE	(842) 7790450
8. PATIENT STATUS	[X] Married
9. OTHER INSURED'S NAME	PALIN KEN D
a. OTHER INSURED'S POLICY OR GROUP NUMBER	568405
b. OTHER INSURED'S DATE OF BIRTH / SEX	02 25 1978 / F [X]
c. EMPLOYER'S NAME OR SCHOOL NAME	BUNYAN UNIVERSITY
d. INSURANCE PLAN NAME OR PROGRAM NAME	CHAMPION INSURANCE
10a. EMPLOYMENT?	[X] NO
10b. AUTO ACCIDENT?	[X] NO
10c. OTHER ACCIDENT?	[X] NO
11. INSURED'S POLICY GROUP OR FECA NUMBER	14980
a. INSURED'S DATE OF BIRTH / SEX	04 18 1972 / M [X]
b. EMPLOYER'S NAME OR SCHOOL NAME	BUNYAN UNIVERSITY
c. INSURANCE PLAN NAME OR PROGRAM NAME	CHAMPION INSURANCE
d. IS THERE ANOTHER HEALTH BENEFIT PLAN?	[X] YES

12. PATIENT'S OR AUTHORIZED PERSON'S SIGNATURE
SIGNED: **SIGNATURE ON FILE**   DATE: 01 20 2009

13. INSURED'S OR AUTHORIZED PERSON'S SIGNATURE
SIGNED: **SIGNATURE ON FILE**

14. DATE OF CURRENT ILLNESS/INJURY/PREGNANCY: 02 13 2009
16. DATES PATIENT UNABLE TO WORK: FROM 02 13 2009 TO 04 19 2009
17. NAME OF REFERRING PROVIDER: **MERIDITH GREY MD**
17b. NPI: 9371048686
18. HOSPITALIZATION DATES: FROM 02 13 2009 TO 02 20 2009
20. OUTSIDE LAB? [X] NO $ CHARGES: 1353

21. DIAGNOSIS OR NATURE OF ILLNESS OR INJURY
1. 719.46
2. 715.96

23. PRIOR AUTHORIZATION NUMBER: 9812375923

#	From	To	POS	CPT/HCPCS	MOD	DX	$ CHARGES	UNITS	NPI
1	01 19 2009	01 19 2009	11	99214	25	1	110 00	1	56446408112
2	01 19 2009	01 19 2009	11	20610	RT	2	125 00	1	56446408112
3	01 19 2009	01 19 2009	11	J7321		2	300 00	1	56446408112

25. FEDERAL TAX I.D. NUMBER: [X] EIN
26. PATIENT'S ACCOUNT NO.: 836135
27. ACCEPT ASSIGNMENT? [X] YES
28. TOTAL CHARGE: $535 00
29. AMOUNT PAID: $0 00
30. BALANCE DUE: $0 00

31. SIGNATURE OF PHYSICIAN OR SUPPLIER: **MERIDITH GREY**   DATE: 01202009

32. SERVICE FACILITY LOCATION:
GARAGE FAMILY PHYSICIANS
1472 FAIRWAY RD
MIDDLETON WI 53562
a. 3030314711

33. BILLING PROVIDER INFO & PH #: (842) 7790450
GARAGE FAMILY PHYSICIANS
1472 FAIRWAY RD
MIDDLETON WI 53562
a. 3030314711

APPROVED OMB-0938-0999 FORM CMS-1500 (08-05)

HEALTH INSURANCE CLAIM FORM

1500
APPROVED BY NATIONAL UNIFORM CLAIM COMMITTEE 08/05

MEDICARE PART B
PO BOX 6704
FARGO, ND 58108-6704

1. MEDICARE [X]	1a. INSURED'S I.D. NUMBER: 094364987D
2. PATIENT'S NAME: BOOP BETTY	3. PATIENT'S BIRTH DATE: 02 14 1940 SEX: F [X]
	4. INSURED'S NAME: BOOP BETTY
5. PATIENT'S ADDRESS: 2468 SUNSET LANE	6. PATIENT RELATIONSHIP TO INSURED: Self [X]
	7. INSURED'S ADDRESS: 2468 SUNSET LANE
CITY: PHOENIX STATE: AZ	8. PATIENT STATUS: Other [X]
	CITY: PHOENIX STATE: AZ
ZIP CODE: 85001 TELEPHONE: (854) 9915151		ZIP CODE: 85001 TELEPHONE: (854) 9915151

9. OTHER INSURED'S NAME:
10. IS PATIENT'S CONDITION RELATED TO:
  a. EMPLOYMENT? NO [X]
  b. AUTO ACCIDENT? NO [X]
  c. OTHER ACCIDENT? NO [X]

11. INSURED'S POLICY GROUP OR FECA NUMBER:
  a. INSURED'S DATE OF BIRTH: 02 14 1940 SEX: F [X]
  b. EMPLOYER'S NAME OR SCHOOL NAME:
  c. INSURANCE PLAN NAME OR PROGRAM NAME: NONE
  d. IS THERE ANOTHER HEALTH BENEFIT PLAN? NO [X]

12. PATIENT'S SIGNATURE: SIGNATURE ON FILE DATE: 0318XXXX
13. INSURED'S SIGNATURE: SIGNATURE ON FILE

14. DATE OF CURRENT ILLNESS/INJURY/PREGNANCY: 03 18 XXXX
17. NAME OF REFERRING PROVIDER:
20. OUTSIDE LAB? $ CHARGES: NONE

21. DIAGNOSIS OR NATURE OF ILLNESS OR INJURY:
1. 290 41
2. 438 00
3. 250 00
4.

24.A. DATE(S) OF SERVICE From / To	B. PLACE OF SERVICE	C. EMG	D. CPT/HCPCS MODIFIER	E. DIAGNOSIS POINTER	F. $ CHARGES	G. DAYS OR UNITS	H. EPSDT	I. ID. QUAL	J. RENDERING PROVIDER ID. #
03 18 XXXX 03 18 XXXX			99308	123	125 00	1		NPI	8415637029

25. FEDERAL TAX I.D. NUMBER: SSN EIN [X]
26. PATIENT'S ACCOUNT NO.: 25641
27. ACCEPT ASSIGNMENT? YES [X]
28. TOTAL CHARGE: $ 125 00
29. AMOUNT PAID: $
30. BALANCE DUE: $ 125 00

31. SIGNATURE OF PHYSICIAN OR SUPPLIER: DEREK SHEPHERD MD DATE: 0318XXXX
32. SERVICE FACILITY LOCATION INFORMATION:
SUN VALLEY NURSING CENTER
2468 SUNSET LANE
PHOENIZ AZ 85001
a. 943628384

33. BILLING PROVIDER INFO & PH #: (854) 9991212
RED ROCK CLINIC
4657 MESA DR
PHOENIX AZ 85002
a. 8415637029

HEALTH INSURANCE CLAIM FORM

1500
APPROVED BY NATIONAL UNIFORM CLAIM COMMITTEE 08/05

CARRIER: BLUE CROSS BLUE SHIELD OF MICHIGAN
600 LAFAYETTE E
DETROIT MI 48226

1. Program: [X] GROUP HEALTH PLAN
1a. INSURED'S I.D. NUMBER: XYZ941275638

2. PATIENT'S NAME: BOONE DANIEL
3. PATIENT'S BIRTH DATE: 11 04 1850 SEX: [X] M
4. INSURED'S NAME: BOONE DANIEL

5. PATIENT'S ADDRESS: 265 MEADOWBROOK LN
CITY: TROY **STATE:** MI
ZIP CODE: 48098 **TELEPHONE:** (213) 8881415

6. PATIENT RELATIONSHIP TO INSURED: [X] Self

7. INSURED'S ADDRESS: 265 MEADOWBROOK LANE
CITY: TROY **STATE:** MI
ZIP CODE: 48098 **TELEPHONE:** (213) 8881415

10. IS PATIENT'S CONDITION RELATED TO:
- a. EMPLOYMENT? [X] NO
- b. AUTO ACCIDENT? [X] NO
- c. OTHER ACCIDENT? (blank)

11. INSURED'S POLICY GROUP OR FECA NUMBER: 81450
a. INSURED'S DATE OF BIRTH: 11 04 1850 SEX: [X] M
c. INSURANCE PLAN NAME OR PROGRAM NAME: NONE
d. IS THERE ANOTHER HEALTH BENEFIT PLAN? [X] NO

12. PATIENT'S SIGNATURE: SIGNATURE ON FILE **DATE:** 0525XXXX
13. INSURED'S SIGNATURE: SIGNATURE ON FILE

14. DATE OF CURRENT: 02 25 XXXX (ILLNESS)
17. NAME OF REFERRING PROVIDER: GREG PRATT MD
17a. GP04768

20. OUTSIDE LAB? $ CHARGES: NONE

21. DIAGNOSIS: 1. 485 00

24. SERVICE LINE 1:
- From: 05 25 XXXX To: 05 25 XXXX
- Place of Service: 23
- CPT/HCPCS: 85025
- $ CHARGES: 75 00
- DAYS/UNITS: 1
- NPI: 753914269

27. ACCEPT ASSIGNMENT? [X] NO

31. SIGNATURE OF PHYSICIAN: ARCHIE MORRIS MD

32. SERVICE FACILITY LOCATION:
NORTH OAKLAND MEDICAL CENTER
461 W HURON ST
PONTIAC MI 48341
a. 9760385412

33. BILLING PROVIDER INFO & PH #: (284) 9991212
ARCHIE MORRIS MD (PATHOLOGY ASSOCIATES)
17564 TELEGRAPH
WEST BLOOMFIELD MI 48378
a. 753914269

APPROVED OMB-0938-0999 FORM CMS-1500 (08-05)

HEALTH INSURANCE CLAIM FORM
1500
APPROVED BY NATIONAL UNIFORM CLAIM COMMITTEE 08/05

BLUE CROSS BLUE SHIELD OF FLORIDA
PO BOX 1798
JACKSONVILLE FL 322310014

PICA | PICA

1. MEDICARE [ ] MEDICAID [ ] TRICARE CHAMPUS [ ] CHAMPVA [ ] GROUP HEALTH PLAN [X] FECA BLK LUNG [ ] OTHER [ ]
1a. INSURED'S I.D. NUMBER: **694712853**

2. PATIENT'S NAME: **BOND JAMES**
3. PATIENT'S BIRTH DATE: **08 07 1950** SEX: M [X] F [ ]
4. INSURED'S NAME: **BOND JAMES**

5. PATIENT'S ADDRESS: **61 MOONRAKER RD**
6. PATIENT RELATIONSHIP TO INSURED: Self [X] Spouse [ ] Child [ ] Other [ ]
7. INSURED'S ADDRESS: **61 MOONRAKER RD**

CITY: **JACKSONVILLE** STATE: **FL**
8. PATIENT STATUS: Single [X] Married [ ] Other [ ]
CITY: **JACKSONVILLE** STATE: **FL**

ZIP CODE: **32231** TELEPHONE: **(999) 5550071**
Employed [ ] Full-Time Student [ ] Part-Time Student [ ]
ZIP CODE: **32231** TELEPHONE: **(999) 5550071**

9. OTHER INSURED'S NAME:
10. IS PATIENT'S CONDITION RELATED TO:
11. INSURED'S POLICY GROUP OR FECA NUMBER:

a. OTHER INSURED'S POLICY OR GROUP NUMBER:
a. EMPLOYMENT? YES [ ] NO [X]
a. INSURED'S DATE OF BIRTH: SEX: M [ ] F [ ]

b. OTHER INSURED'S DATE OF BIRTH: SEX: M [ ] F [ ]
b. AUTO ACCIDENT? YES [ ] NO [X] PLACE (State):
b. EMPLOYER'S NAME OR SCHOOL NAME:

c. EMPLOYER'S NAME OR SCHOOL NAME:
c. OTHER ACCIDENT? YES [ ] NO [X]
c. INSURANCE PLAN NAME OR PROGRAM NAME: **NONE**

d. INSURANCE PLAN NAME OR PROGRAM NAME:
10d. RESERVED FOR LOCAL USE:
d. IS THERE ANOTHER HEALTH BENEFIT PLAN? YES [ ] NO [X]

12. PATIENT'S OR AUTHORIZED PERSON'S SIGNATURE
SIGNED: **SIGNATURE ON FILE** DATE: **0709XXXX**
13. INSURED'S OR AUTHORIZED PERSON'S SIGNATURE
SIGNED: **SIGNATURE ON FILE**

14. DATE OF CURRENT: **02 15 XXXX** ILLNESS/INJURY/PREGNANCY
15. IF PATIENT HAS HAD SAME OR SIMILAR ILLNESS:
16. DATES PATIENT UNABLE TO WORK IN CURRENT OCCUPATION: FROM TO

17. NAME OF REFERRING PROVIDER OR OTHER SOURCE: **GEORGE BAILEY**
17a. **GB74625**
17b. NPI
18. HOSPITALIZATION DATES RELATED TO CURRENT SERVICES: FROM TO

19. RESERVED FOR LOCAL USE
20. OUTSIDE LAB? YES [ ] NO [ ] $ CHARGES: **NONE**

21. DIAGNOSIS OR NATURE OF ILLNESS OR INJURY:
1. **719 41**
2.
3.
4.

22. MEDICAID RESUBMISSION CODE: ORIGINAL REF. NO.
23. PRIOR AUTHORIZATION NUMBER

24.
#	From	To	POS	EMG	CPT/HCPCS	MODIFIER	DX	$ CHARGES	UNITS	EPSDT	ID QUAL	RENDERING PROVIDER ID #
1	07 09 XXXX	07 09 XXXX	49		73223	LT 26	1	1500 00	1		NPI	8476293517
2											NPI	
3											NPI	
4											NPI	
5											NPI	
6											NPI	

25. FEDERAL TAX I.D. NUMBER: **3897172465** SSN [ ] EIN [X]
26. PATIENT'S ACCOUNT NO.:
27. ACCEPT ASSIGNMENT? YES [X] NO [ ]
28. TOTAL CHARGE: $ **1500 00**
29. AMOUNT PAID: $
30. BALANCE DUE: $ **1500 00**

31. SIGNATURE OF PHYSICIAN OR SUPPLIER:
MIRANDA BAILEY MD DATE: **0709XXXX**

32. SERVICE FACILITY LOCATION INFORMATION:
ULTRACARE IMAGING SERVICE
4610 W HILLSBORO BLVD
COCONUT CREEK FL 33073
a. **9537421683**

33. BILLING PROVIDER INFO & PH #: **(915) 4421833**
MIRANDA BAILEY MD
4310 W HILLSBORO BLVD
COCONUT CREEK FL 33073
a. **8476293517**

APPROVED OMB-0938-0999 FORM CMS-1500 (08-05)

HEALTH INSURANCE CLAIM FORM
1500
APPROVED BY NATIONAL UNIFORM CLAIM COMMITTEE 08/05

CARRIER: UNITED HEALTH CARE, 450 COLUMBUS BLVD, HARTFORD CT 06103

1. Type	GROUP HEALTH PLAN (X)
1a. INSURED'S I.D. NUMBER	694712853
2. PATIENT'S NAME	EWING JOHN R
3. PATIENT'S BIRTH DATE / SEX	12 10 1950 M (X)
4. INSURED'S NAME	EWING JOHN R
5. PATIENT'S ADDRESS	4546 DALLAS DR
CITY / STATE	SAN FRANCISCO / CA
ZIP CODE	92564
TELEPHONE	(901) 5452212
6. PATIENT RELATIONSHIP TO INSURED	Self (X)
7. INSURED'S ADDRESS	4546 DALLAS DR
CITY / STATE	SAN FRANCISCO / CA
ZIP CODE	92564
TELEPHONE	(901) 5452212
8. PATIENT STATUS	Single (X)
10a. EMPLOYMENT?	NO (X)
10b. AUTO ACCIDENT?	NO (X)
10c. OTHER ACCIDENT?	NO (X)
11. INSURED'S POLICY GROUP OR FECA NUMBER	9897
11a. INSURED'S DATE OF BIRTH / SEX	12 10 1950 M (X)
11d. IS THERE ANOTHER HEALTH BENEFIT PLAN?	NO (X)
12. PATIENT'S SIGNATURE	SIGNATURE ON FILE — DATE 0412XXXX
13. INSURED'S SIGNATURE	SIGNATURE ON FILE
14. DATE OF CURRENT ILLNESS	03 10 XXXX
17. NAME OF REFERRING PROVIDER	GEORGE BAILEY
17b. NPI	5126487930
20. OUTSIDE LAB?	NO — $ CHARGES NONE
21. DIAGNOSIS	1. 724 30 2. 719 45

24. Service Lines

#	From (MM DD YY)	To (MM DD YY)	POS	CPT/HCPCS	DX PTR	$ CHARGES	DAYS/UNITS	NPI
1	04 12 XXXX	04 12 XXXX	49	97035	12	300 00	2	5126487930
2	04 12 XXXX	04 12 XXXX	49	97140	1	100 00	1	5126487930
3	04 12 XXXX	04 12 XXXX	49	97110	12	100 00	2	5126487930
4	04 12 XXXX	04 12 XXXX	49	97034	12	75 00	12	5126487930

25. FEDERAL TAX I.D. NUMBER	381796542 (EIN X)
27. ACCEPT ASSIGNMENT?	YES (X)
28. TOTAL CHARGE	$ 575 00
29. AMOUNT PAID	$
30. BALANCE DUE	$ 575 00
31. SIGNATURE OF PHYSICIAN	BARB MARTIN RPT 0810XXXX
32. SERVICE FACILITY	NOVA CARE PHYSICAL THERAPY, 3678 OAKLAND BLVD, SAN FRANCISCO CA 92564 — a. 0914287356
33. BILLING PROVIDER	NOVA CARE PHYSICAL THERAPY CENTER, 3678 OAKLAND BLVD, SAN FRANCISCO CA 92564 — (901) 5558412 — a. 0914287356

1

2

3a PAT. CNTL #

b. MED. REC. #

4 TYPE OF BILL

5 FED. TAX NO.

6 STATEMENT COVERS PERIOD FROM THROUGH

7

8 PATIENT NAME a

b

9 PATIENT ADDRESS a

b c d e

10 BIRTHDATE | 11 SEX | ADMISSION 12 DATE 13 HR 14 TYPE 15 SRC | 16 DHR | 17 STAT | CONDITION CODES 18 19 20 21 22 23 24 25 26 27 28 | 29 ACDT STATE | 30

31 OCCURRENCE CODE DATE | 32 OCCURRENCE CODE DATE | 33 OCCURRENCE CODE DATE | 34 OCCURRENCE CODE DATE | 35 OCCURRENCE SPAN CODE FROM THROUGH | 36 OCCURRENCE SPAN CODE FROM THROUGH | 37

a
b

38

39 VALUE CODES CODE AMOUNT | 40 VALUE CODES CODE AMOUNT | 41 VALUE CODES CODE AMOUNT

a
b
c
d

42 REV. CD.	43 DESCRIPTION	44 HCPCS / RATE / HIPPS CODE	45 SERV. DATE	46 SERV. UNITS	47 TOTAL CHARGES	48 NON-COVERED CHARGES	49
1							1
2							2
3							3
4							4
5							5
6							6
7							7
8							8
9							9
10							10
11							11
12							12
13							13
14							14
15							15
16							16
17							17
18							18
19							19
20							20
21							21
22							22
23	***PAGE ____ OF ____***	***CREATION DATE***		***TOTALS***			23

50 PAYER NAME | 51 HEALTH PLAN ID | 52 REL. INFO | 53 ASG. BEN. | 54 PRIOR PAYMENTS | 55 EST. AMOUNT DUE | 56 NPI

A
B
C

57 OTHER PRV ID

58 INSURED'S NAME | 59 P.REL | 60 INSURED'S UNIQUE ID | 61 GROUP NAME | 62 INSURANCE GROUP NO.

A
B
C

63 TREATMENT AUTHORIZATION CODES | 64 DOCUMENT CONTROL NUMBER | 65 EMPLOYER NAME

A
B
C

66 DX 67 A B C D E F G H 68

I J K L M N O P Q

69 ADMIT DX | 70 PATIENT REASON DX a b c | 71 PPS CODE | 72 ECI a b c | 73

74 PRINCIPAL PROCEDURE CODE DATE | a. OTHER PROCEDURE CODE DATE | b. OTHER PROCEDURE CODE DATE | 75

c. OTHER PROCEDURE CODE DATE | d. OTHER PROCEDURE CODE DATE | e. OTHER PROCEDURE CODE DATE

76 ATTENDING NPI QUAL
LAST FIRST

77 OPERATING NPI QUAL
LAST FIRST

80 REMARKS

81CC a
b
c
d

78 OTHER NPI QUAL
LAST FIRST

79 OTHER NPI QUAL
LAST FIRST

UB-04 CMS-1450 APPROVED OMB NO. 0938-0997 NUBC National Uniform Billing Committee

THE CERTIFICATIONS ON THE REVERSE APPLY TO THIS BILL AND ARE MADE A PART HEREOF.

HEALTH INSURANCE CLAIM FORM

APPROVED BY NATIONAL UNIFORM CLAIM COMMITTEE 08/05

MEDICARE PART B
PO BOX 5555
MARION IL 62959

1. MEDICARE [X] (Medicare #)
1a. INSURED'S I.D. NUMBER: 425378961A

2. PATIENT'S NAME: MARTIN JOSEPH
3. PATIENT'S BIRTH DATE: 09 15 1940 SEX: M [X]
4. INSURED'S NAME: MARTIN JOSEPH

5. PATIENT'S ADDRESS: 7679 WILLSHIRE BLVD
6. PATIENT RELATIONSHIP TO INSURED: Self [X]
7. INSURED'S ADDRESS: 7679 WILLSHIRE BLVD

CITY: CHICAGO STATE: IL
8. PATIENT STATUS: Other [X]
CITY: CHICAGO STATE: IL

ZIP CODE: 62946 TELEPHONE: (319) 6151212
ZIP CODE: 62946 TELEPHONE: (319) 6151212

10. IS PATIENT'S CONDITION RELATED TO:
a. EMPLOYMENT? NO [X]
b. AUTO ACCIDENT? NO [X]
c. OTHER ACCIDENT? NO [X]

11. INSURED'S POLICY GROUP OR FECA NUMBER:
a. INSURED'S DATE OF BIRTH: 09 15 1940 SEX: M [X]

d. IS THERE ANOTHER HEALTH BENEFIT PLAN? NO [X]

12. PATIENT'S OR AUTHORIZED PERSON'S SIGNATURE
SIGNED: SIGNATURE ON FILE   DATE: 1010XXXX

13. INSURED'S OR AUTHORIZED PERSON'S SIGNATURE
SIGNED: SIGNATURE ON FILE

14. DATE OF CURRENT: 10 10 XXXX ILLNESS (First symptom) OR INJURY (Accident) OR PREGNANCY (LMP)

20. OUTSIDE LAB? $ CHARGES: NONE

21. DIAGNOSIS OR NATURE OF ILLNESS OR INJURY:
1. 427.10
2. 427.31

24. A. DATE(S) OF SERVICE From — To	B. PLACE OF SERVICE	C. EMG	D. CPT/HCPCS	MODIFIER	E. DIAGNOSIS POINTER	F. $ CHARGES	G. DAYS OR UNITS	H.	I. ID. QUAL	J. RENDERING PROVIDER ID. #
1	10 10 XXXX 10 10 XXXX	22		93620	26	12	1500 00	1		NPI	9071826354
2	10 10 XXXX 10 10 XXXX	22		93609	26	12	900 00	1		NPI	

25. FEDERAL TAX I.D. NUMBER: 38724956 [X] EIN
27. ACCEPT ASSIGNMENT? NO [X]
28. TOTAL CHARGE: $ 2400 00
30. BALANCE DUE: $ 2400 00

31. SIGNATURE OF PHYSICIAN OR SUPPLIER
SIGNED: CHRISTINA YANG MD DATE: 1010XXXX

32. SERVICE FACILITY LOCATION INFORMATION:
NORTHWESTERN UNIVERSITY HOSPITAL
13789 MICHIGAN AVE
CHICAGO IL 62957
a. 8975312640

33. BILLING PROVIDER INFO & PH #: (314) 5151459
CHRISTINA YANG MD (YANG HART ASSOCIATION)
13752 MICHIGAN AVE
CHICAGO IL 62957
a. 9071826354

157

Fee Schedule

Department	CPT Code	Description	Price
Evaluation and Management	99201	New Patient Office Visit - Level 1	$100.00
	99202	New Patient Office Visit - Level 2	$120.00
	99203	New Patient Office Visit - Level 3	$140.00
	99204	New Patient Office Visit - Level 4	$150.00
	99205	New Patient Office Visit - Level 5	$160.00
	99211	Est. Patient Office Visit - Level 1	$75.00
	99212	Est. Patient Office Visit - Level 2	$95.00
	99213	Est. Patient Office Visit - Level 3	$115.00
	99214	Est. Patient Office Visit - Level 4	$135.00
	99215	Est. Patient Office Visit - Level 5	$155.00
Surgery - Integumentary	10060	Incision and drainage of abscess	$195.00
	10080	Incision and drainage of pilonidal cyst	$250.00
	10120	Incision and drainage of hematoma, seroma, or fluid collection	$275.00
	10160	Puncture aspiration of abscess	$150.00
	11200	Removal of skin tags; up to 15	$70.00
	+11201	Each addiotnal 10 skin tags	$30.00
Surgery - Respiratory	30100	Biopsy, intranasal	$185.00
	30110	Excision, nasal polyp(s)	$135.00
	32035	Thoracostomy with rib resection for empyema	$542.00
	32200	Pneumonostomy with drainage of abscess	$1,300.00
	32440	Total pneumonectomy	$1,750.00
Surgery - Cardiovascular	33206	Insertion or replacement of permanent pacemaker	$750.00
	33210	Insertion or replacement of temporary pacemaker	$550.00
	33500	Repair of coronary arteriocenous chamber	$975.00
	33510	Coronary artery bypass, vein only	$2,500.00
Surgery - Digestive	40500	Vermilionectomy	$375.00
	40650	Repair lip, full thickness, vermilion only	$250.00
	40830	Closure of laceration 2.5 cm- on vestibule	$95.00
	40831	Closure of laceration 2.6 cm+ on vestibule	$130.00
	43500	Gastromy; with exploration	$375.00
Radiology	73500	Hip; single unilateral x-ray	$45.00
	73510	Hip; minimum two complete view x-ray	$55.00
	74000	Abdominal; single anterposterior x-ray	$45.00
	74150	Abdominal; Tomography w/out contrast	$125.00
Pathology	80048	Basic metabolic panel (Calcium, total)	$65.00
	80051	Electrolyte panel	$45.00
	80100	Drug screen; qualitative	$20.00
	81000	Urinalysis	$20.00
	85025	Complete Blood Count	$60.00

Your Name and Logo Goes Here

Superbill #

Your Address and Phone Numbers

CPT	DESCRIPTION	DX	FEE
	NEW PATIENT		
99201	Minimal Office Visit		65
99202	Focused Office Visit		85
99203	Expanded Office Visit		125
99204	Detailed Office Visit		165
99205	Comp. Office Visit		215
	ESTABLISHED PATIENT		
99211	Minimal Office Visit		30
99212	Focused Office Visit		55
99213	Expanded Office Visit		80
99214	Detailed Office Visit		110
99215	Comp. Office Visit		175
	NEW PATIENT		
99381	Prevent., Under Age		130
99382	Preventative, Age 1-4		150
99383	Preventative, Age 5-11		150
99384	Prevent., Age 12-17		165
	ESTABLISHED PATIENT		
99391	Prevent., Under Age		115
99392	Preventative, Age 1-4		130
99393	Preventative, Age 5-11		130
99394	Prevent., Age 12-17		150
	OFFICE CONSULTS		
99241	Focused		83
99242	Expanded		114
99243	Detailed		141
99244	Comprehensive		174
99245	Complex		242

CPT	DESCRIPTION	DX	FEE
	INJECTIONS		
90471	Admin., First Injection		17
90472	Admin., Subsequent		17
90633	Hepatitis A	V06.1	80
90647	HiB	V03.81	40
90657	Influenza, 6-35 Mos.	V04.81	15
90658	Influenza, 3-21 Years	V04.81	15
90669	Pneumococcal	V03.82	100
90700	DTaP	V06.1	35
90707	MMR	V06.4	60
90710	Pro Quad	V06.8	155
90713	Poliovirus	V04.0	40
90716	Varicella Virus	V05.4	95
90714	TD Over Age 7	V06.5	20
90715	Tdap - Boostrix	V06.1	70
90744	Hep B, Pediatric/Adoles.	V05.3	40
90734	Menactra	V03.89	160
90733	Menomune	V03.89	100
90723	Pediarix	V06.8	100
86580	TB Intradermal	V74.1	25
90772	Antibiotic Injection		26
95115	Allergy - Single Injection		20
95117	Allergy - Two +		45
J0696	Rocephin 250 mg		35

CPT	DESCRIPTION	DX	FEE
	LAB SERVICES		
82270	Hemocult		10
81002	Urinalysis, w/o		15
85025	Hemogram, CBC		25
86403	Rapid Strep		25
86308	Monospot		15
82948	Glucometer Strip		10
81025	Pregnancy Test, Urine		25
36415	Venipuncture		15
	OTHER SERVICES		
94760	Blood Oxygen Level		25
94761	Blood Oxygen Level		45
12001	Repair Superficial Wound		155
12011	Repair Superficial Face		180
16000	Initial, 1st Degree Burn		108
17250	Chem. Cauterization		75
69200	Remove Foreign Body		105
69210	Impacted Cerumen		70
92567	Tympanometry		35
94640	Inhal. Treatment		40
94640-76	Subs. Inhal. Treatment		40
99173	Vision		25
92551	Pure Tone Hearing, Air		35
99429	Sports Physical		35
10060	Incision & Drainage		125
17110	Cryotherapy/Wart Destruction		100
99050	Services After Hours		30
99054	Services on Sunday/Holiday		45
99078	Physician Educational Service		65

#	Diagnosis	ICD-9	Modifier
1			
2			
3			
4			
5			
6			

NEXT VISIT: _____ Days _____ Weeks _____ Months M.D. _____ Vaccine _____

Today's Date		New Patient? ☐ Yes ☐ No	Today's Charges $
Patient's Name		DOB / /	Today's Payments $
Primary Ins	Secondary Ins	Sex	Cash
Primary Ins #	Secondary Ins #	Co-Pay	Check No. / Charge

Revised 9-26-8

Attachment C – Valid Revenue Codes

Revcode	Description
258	Pharmacy – IV Solutions
259	Pharmacy – Other Pharmacy
260	IV Therapy – General classification
261	IV Therapy – Infusion Pump
262	IV Therapy – Pharmacy Svcs
263	IV Therapy – Drug/Supply Delivery
264	IV Therapy – Supplies
269	IV Therapy – Other
270	Medical/Surgical Supplies and Devices – General Classification
271	Medical/Surgical Supplies and Devices – Non Sterile
272	Medical/Surgical Supplies and Devices – Sterile
273	Medical/Surgical Supplies and Devices – Take Home
274	Medical/Surgical Supplies and Devices – Prosthetic/Orthotic Devices
275	Medical/Surgical Supplies and Devices – Pace Maker
276	Medical/Surgical Supplies and Devices – Intraocular Lens
277	Medical/Surgical Supplies and Devices – Oxygen – Take Home
278	Medical/Surgical Supplies and Devices – Other Implants
279	Medical/Surgical Supplies and Devices – Other Supplies/Devices
280	Oncology – General Classification
289	Oncology – Other
290	Durable Medical Equipment – General Classification
291	Durable Medical Equipment – Rental
292	Durable Medical Equipment – Purchase of new DME
293	Durable Medical Equipment – Purchase of used DME
294	Durable Medical Equipment – Supplies/Drugs for DME Effectiveness
299	Durable Medical Equipment – Other Equipment
300	Laboratory – General Classification
301	Laboratory – Chemistry
302	Laboratory – Immunologu
303	Laboratory – Renal Patient (Home)
304	Laboratory – Non-Routine Dialysis
305	Laboratory – Hematology
306	Laboratory – Bacteriology and Microbiology
307	Laboratory – Urology
309	Laboratory – Other
310	Laboratory Pathological – General Classification
311	Laboratory Pathological – Cytology
312	Laboratory Pathological – Histology
314	Laboratory Pathological – Biopsy
319	Laboratory Pathological – Other
320	Radiology Diagnostic – General Classification
321	Radiology Diagnostic – Angiocardiography
322	Radiology Diagnostic – Arthography
323	Radiology Diagnostic – Arterlography
324	Radiology Diagnostic – Chest X-Ray
329	Radiology Diagnostic – Other
330	Radiology Therapeutic – General Classification
331	Radiology Therapeutic – Chemotherapy – Injected
332	Radiology Therapeutic – Chemotherapy – Oral
333	Radiology Therapeutic – Radiation Therapy
335	Radiology Therapeutic – Chemotherapy – IV
339	Radiology Therapeutic – Other
340	Nuclear Medicine – General Classification
341	Nuclear Medicine – Diagnostic
342	Nuclear Medicine - Therapeutic

018500   HOSP09715

STATEMENT

PAYMENTS MADE AFTER 04/08/2007 WILL APPEAR ON NEXT STATEMENT. QUESTIONS REGARDING THIS INVOICE CATN BE DIRECTED TO THE OFFICE BETWEEN 1:00PM AND 4:00PM DAILY

ADDRESS SERVICE REQUESTED

SHOW AMOUNT PAID HERE $ _____

168.12 PATIENT BALANCE

05/04/07   01

OFFICE PHONE   CLOSING DATE   YOUR ACCOUNT   PAGE NO.

NOTE: Charges and payments not appearing on this statement will appear on next month's statement.

PLEASE RETURN THIS PORTION WITH PAYMENT

CHARGES APPEARING ON THIS STATEMENT ARE NOT INCLUDED ON ANY HOSPITAL BILL OR STATEMENT

DATE	PROVIDER	EXPLANATION OF ACTIVITY	PATIENT NAME	CHARGES AND DEBTS	PAYMENTS & CREDITS
072905		INITIAL INPTH COMP HISTORY		365.00	
073005		FOLLOW CONSULT		250.00	
060205		MEDICARE #11545 FILED			
092605		PAYMENT MEDICARE C# 115451			-291.17
092605		WRITE-OFF MEDICARE C# 115451			-251.04
092605		CO-INS 72.79			
080105		FOLLOW UP CONSULATATION		720.00	
060205		MEDICARE #11546 FILED			
092405		PAYMENT MEDICARE C# 115461			-319.68
092405		PAYMENT MEDICARE C# 115461			-320.40
092405		CO-INS 79.92			
080905		HOSPITAL DISCHARGE MGMT.		100.00	
060205		MEDICARE #11547 FILED			-61.64
092605		PAYMENT MEDICARE C# 115471			-22.95
092605		WRITE-OFF MEDICARE C#115471			
092605		CO-INS 15.41			

STATEMENT CLOSING DATE   **05/04/07**   PLEASE INDICATE YOUR ACCOUNT NUMBER WHEN CALLING OUR OFFICE.

CURRENT	30-60 DAYS	60-90 DAYS	> 90 DAYS	TOTAL	INS. PENDING	PATIENT BALANCE FOR THIS AMOUNT
			168.12	168.12	0.00	168.12

SEND INQUIRIES TO:

PATIENT INFORMATION

YOUR NAME: _____
          (FIRST)   (MIDDLE)   (LAST)

BIRTH DATE: _____ SEX: MALE___ FEMALE___ S.S.#:____-___-____

MARITAL STATUS: S___ M___ D___ W___ HOME PHONE #: (___)____-____

HOME ADDRESS:_____

CITY:_____ STATE:_____ ZIP CODE:_____

EMPLOYER:_____ WK PHONE: (___)____-____

NAME OF SPOUSE:_____ BIRTH DATE: ___/___/____

SPOUSE'S SOCIAL SECURITY #:____-___-____ WORK PHONE: (___)____-____

****

IN CASE OF EMERGENCY CONTACT (NAME)_____
                                             (FIRST)   (LAST)

RELATIONSHIP TO PATIENT:_____ HOME PHONE #: (___)____-____

WORK PHONE: (___)____-____

PLEASE SEE OTHER SIDE

FINANCIAL AGREEMENT

1. Payment in full is due at the time. We accept cash, checks, VISA, MasterCard or Discover cards. Your insurance coverage is not a guarantee of payment. Your **insurance carrier may decide that the services that were rendered were not medically necessary or not a covered benefit** and they **may not pay the** claim. Any balance not paid by your insurance carrier will be your responsibility.

2. All Co-Pays must be paid in full at the time of service. The co-pay amount is set by a contract between you and your insurance carrier. Failure to pay your co-pay at the time of service will force us to contact your insurance carrier that you are not compliant with your contract with them.

3. If your insurance company requires that lab work or specimens need to be sent to a specific laboratory, it is YOUR responsibility to know which laboratory your insurance company participates with. It is also your responsibility to let our office know which lab.

4. In the case of estranged or divorced parents, the custodial parent is responsible for payment for all services rendered, **regardless of any insurance arrangements or divorce decree**. This is per the law from the State of Michigan regarding minor children. We will gladly furnish a receipt when payment is made by you so that you can turn this into friend of the court.

5. If you are experiencing financial difficulties, please talk to our billing department at _____ or our office manager, in order to arrange a suitable payment schedule.

6. The physicians are not experts on the many insurance contracts and cannot be aware of all financial arrangements. Please discuss all insurance problems and financial issues with our billing department at _____ or speak with our office manager.

7. All accounts overdue by more than 90 days may be turned over to a collection agency. If your insurance company has not paid your claim within 120 days the balance will be turned over to you for payment. Our past experience now requires us to adopt this policy in order to stay in business.

8. **There is an additional $25.00 returned check fee added plus the amount of your check** to your account in addition to the amount of your check that did not clear.

9. **When you do not call to cancel your appointment 24 hours in advance there will be a $25.00 NO SHOW fee added to your account.**

I UNDERSTAND AND ACCEPT THE ABOVE STATEMENTS.

_____   _____
PATIENT OR DPOA OR Guardian   Date

1 Faith United Hospital 700 LaCross Ave City XX 12345 9892223333	2		3a PAT. CNTL # 525252 b. MED. REC. # 555999		4 TYPE OF BILL 0131
		5 FED. TAX NO. 12-3456789	6 STATEMENT COVERS PERIOD FROM 011907 THROUGH 012007	7	

8 PATIENT NAME b STRONG WENDY	9 PATIENT ADDRESS b DETROIT	a 2014 ANNIE ST	c MI	d 48234	e

10 BIRTHDATE 07241951	11 SEX F	12 DATE 011907	13 HR 22	14 TYPE 2	15 SRC 1	16 DHR 04	17 STAT 01	18-28 CONDITION CODES	29 ACDT STATE	30

Charges

42 REV. CD.	43 DESCRIPTION	44 HCPCS/RATE/HIPPS CODE	45 SERV. DATE	46 SERV. UNITS	47 TOTAL CHARGES	48 NON-COVERED CHARGES
0300	LAB	80101	011907	1	65 00	
0300	LAB	82055	011907	1	60 00	
0300	LAB	86001	011907	1	1269 00	
0637	DRUG/SELF ADMIN	9928525	011907	1	5 12	5 12
0001	TOTAL CHARGES				1434 00	5 12
	PAGE 1 OF 1	CREATION DATE 012507	TOTALS		1434 00	5 12

50 PAYER NAME A MEDICARE	51 HEALTH PLAN ID XXX	52 REL INFO Y	53 ASG BEN Y	54 PRIOR PAYMENTS	55 EST. AMOUNT DUE	56 NPI 1234512345 57 OTHER PRV ID 999888

58 INSURED'S NAME A STRONG WENDY	59 P.REL 18	60 INSURED'S UNIQUE ID 333222555	61 GROUP NAME	62 INSURANCE GROUP NO.

63 TREATMENT AUTHORIZATION CODES	64 DOCUMENT CONTROL NUMBER	65 EMPLOYER NAME

66 DX	67 311	A 3008	B 30500	C 4019	D	E	F	G	H	68

69 ADMIT DX 3008	70 PATIENT REASON DX	71 PPS CODE	72 ECI	73

74 PRINCIPAL PROCEDURE CODE/DATE	OTHER PROCEDURE CODE/DATE	75	76 ATTENDING NPI 111122222 LAST LUCIDO	QUAL 1G UP1234 FIRST MARY JO
			77 OPERATING NPI LAST	QUAL FIRST
80 REMARKS	81CC a b c d		78 OTHER NPI LAST 79 OTHER NPI LAST	QUAL FIRST QUAL FIRST

UB-04 CMS-1450   APPROVED OMB NO. 0938-0997   NUBC National Uniform Billing Committee   THE CERTIFICATIONS ON THE REVERSE APPLY TO THIS BILL AND ARE MADE A PART HEREOF.

WISCONSIN PHYSICIAN SERVICES
PO BOX 5555
MARION IL 62959
866-234-7331

MEDICARE
REMITTANCE
NOTICE

MARSHA BROOKS MD
503 MEDICAL TOWERS
TROY MI 48098

PROVIDER #:   0352681
PAGE #:   1 OF 1
DATE: 0813xxxx
CHECK/EFT #: 560784

PERF PROV	SERV DATE	POS NOS	PROC	MODS	BILLED	ALLOWED	DEDUCT	COINS	GRP/RC	– AMT	PROV PD
NAME	GRAHAM MITCHELL		HIC 392594611A	ACNT	CASE C-14	ICN	1234679			ASGY	MAO MAO1
0352681	0714 0714xxxx	11 001	99205		200.00	188.07	0.00	37.61	CO-42	11.93	150.46
	0714 0714xxxx	11 001	81001		15.00	5.25	0.00	1.05	CO-42	4.75	4.20
PT RESP	38.66		CLAIM TOTAL		215.00	193.32		38.66		16.68	154.66
ADJS: PREVS PD	0.00	PD TO BENE	0.00	INT	0.00	PRIMARY	0.00			OTHER	0.00
										154.66	NET
NAME	JOHNSTONE MARY ALICE		HIC 292995651c1	ACNT	CASE 13	ICN	1234680			ASGY	MA0 MA01
0352681	0724 0724xxxx	11 001	99205		200.00	188.07	0.00	37.61	CO-42	11.93	150.46
M34	0724 0724xxxx	11 001	84443		15.00	15.00	0.00		CO-17		
	0724 0724xxxx	11 001	84480		20.00	9.75	0.00	1.95	CO-42	10.25	7.80
PT RESP	22.18		CLAIM TOTAL		235.00	212.82		41.51		22.18	158.26
ADJS: PREVS PD	0.00	PD TO BENE	0.00	INT	0.00	PRIMARY	0.00			OTHER	0.00
										158.26	NET
NAME	POWELL BRANDON		HIC 372529175A	ACNT	CASE 15	ICN	1234681			ASG Y	MAO MA01
0352681	0714 0714xxxx	22 001	93510		500.00	280.35	0.00	56.07	CO-42	219.65	224.28
	0714 0714xxxx	22 001	93545		30.00	16.97	0.00	3.39	CO-42	13.03	13.58
	0714 0714xxxx	22 001	93543		35.00	22.80	0.00	4.56	CO-42	12.20	18.24
	0714 0714xxxx	22 001	93555		50.00	48.04	0.00	9.61	CO-42	1.96	38.43
	0714 0714xxxx	22 001	93556		55.00	49.21	0.00	5.84	CO-42	5.79	43.37
PT RESP	79.47		CLAIM TOTAL		670.00	417.37		79.47		252.63	337.90
ADJS: PREVS PD	0.00	PD TO BENE	0.00	INT	0.00	PRIMARY	0.00			OTHER	0.00
CLAIM TRANSFERRED TO BCBS										337.90	NET

TOTALS	TOTAL CLAIMS	TOTAL BILLED	TOTAL ALLOWED	TOTAL DEDUCT	TOTAL COINS	TOTAL RC AMT	TOTAL PROV PD
	3	1120.00	808.51		157.69	291.49	650.82
ADJS	TOTAL PREV PD	TOTAL PD TO BENE	TOTAL INT	TOTAL PRIMARY	TOTAL OFFSET	TOTAL OTHER ADJS	AMOUNT OF CHECK
	0.00	0.00	0.00	0.00	0.00	0.00	650.82

GLOSSARY: GROUP, REASON, MOA AND REMARK CODES

CO   CONTRACTUAL OBLIGATION. AMOUNT FOR WHICH THE PROVIDE IS FINANCIALLY LIABLE. THE PATIENT MAY NOT BE
            BILLED FOR THIS AMOUNT.
42   CHARGES EXCEED OUR FEE SCHEDULE OR MAXIMUM ALLOWABLE AMOUNT

MA01   IF YOU DO NOT AGREE WITH WHAT WE APPROVED FOR THESE SERVICES, YOU MAY APPEAL OUR DECISION. TO MAKE
            SURE THAT WE ARE FAIR TO YOU, WE REQUIRE ANOTHER INDIVIDUAL THAT DID NOT PROCESS YOU INTIAL CLAIM TO
            CONDUCT THE REVIEW. HOWEVER, IN ORDER TO BE ELIGIBLE FOR A REVIEW, YOU MUST WRITE TO US WITHIN 120 DAYS
            OF THE DATE OF THIS NOTICE, UNLESS YOU HAVE A GOOD REASON FOR BEING LATE.

Global Insurance Co.
PO Box 3000
Grand Rapids MI 49175

EXPLANATION OF BENEFITS
PLEASE RETAIN FOR FUTURE REFERENCE

Date Printed – 8/25/xxxx
Tax ID #: 344102810
Check #: 3565987234
Check Amt: $

Marvin Klein MD
515 Somerset
Troy, MI 48098

Notes: The benefits listed below reflect your portion of this payment.

Patient Name: Joseph Martino
Patient Acct #: Case # 2 Patient ID# 2145556
Member ID # 342556630
Relation: Self   Member: Joseph

Service Dates	CPT Codes	PL	NUM SVC	Submitted Charges	Copay Amount	Not Payable	See Remarks	Deduct	Co-Insurance	Patient Responsible	Payable Amount
07/13/xx	99202	11	1	$75.00				$75.00		$75.00	
07/13/xx	93000	11	1	$45.00							$45.00
TOTALS				$120.00				$75.00		$75.00	$45.00

For Questions regarding this claim Call 888-6539797 For Assistance. Please use ID number for reference to this claim	Total Patient Responsibility	$75.00

TCF Bank   Check #: 3567895234
56624 Highland Rd
Waterford MI 48327   8/25/xxxx

PAY FORTY FIVE AND NO/100**

******** $45.00

TO THE ODER OF:
MARVIN KLEIN MD
515 SOMERSET
TROY MI 48098

Nicholas Jones

```
[RP009321] Insurance                                                    DATE   1/28/2009
GARAGE FAMILY PHYSICIANS        Aged Outstanding Claims                 TIME     14:45
USER - MLS                                                              PAGE         1
```

CLAIM #	PATIENT #	PATIENT NAME			DATE FILED	DATE REFILED	DATE OF SERVICE	CURRENT	31-60	61-90	90+	B [AGE] I
564889	58680	STEVENSON	ROBERT	M	01/03/08		12/07/07				68.00	390
232354	546882	DARLING	WENDY	K	01/03/08	01/15/09	06/02/08				270.00	237
357512	755588	SCHMIDT	KATIE	J	10/16/08		09/24/08				82.00	103
314854	68144	FISCHER	CARRIE	A	11/03/08		11/03/08			74.00		85
355568	152235	SAN DIEGO	CARMEN	L	11/13/08		10/30/08			74.00		75
535541	55422	STEIN	FRANKEN	D	11/26/08		11/06/08			145.00		62
535545	579869	POOKA	HARVEY	A	12/08/08	01/15/09	12/05/08		74.00			50
598878	684489	GABRIEL	LOLA	F	12/15/08		11/24/08		155.00			43
354875	900846	WESTSIDE	MARIA	C	12/29/08		12/23/08	74.00				29
546688	578880	ADAMS	EVA	E	01/08/09		01/06/09	178.00				20
648500	586687	NARIZ	BELLA	L	01/15/09		10/29/07	205.00				13

```
INS CO# 2 MEDICARE       PHONE # 313 225 8222      TOTAL    CURRENT   31-60    61-90   OVER 90
                         11 CLAIMS TOTALING      1,399.00    457.00  229.00   293.00    420.00
```

CLAIM #	PATIENT #	PATIENT NAME			DATE FILED	DATE REFILED	DATE OF SERVICE	CURRENT	31-60	61-90	90+	B [AGE] I
946540	315540	OZ	DOROTHY	M	12/17/06	05/14/08	03/30/06				50.00	772
235008	350005	MENACE	DENNIS	K	08/08/07		08/21/07				68.00	538
564658	135849	BULLOCK	SANDRA	J	05/16/08		05/01/08				150.00	256
435689	54611	TOMATO	ROMANO	A	11/10/08		11/03/08			74.00		78
955400	564604	DRUNKARD	BACHUS	L	01/20/09		01/20/09	74.00				8
984050	468764	MANN	ILOVE	D	01/22/09		01/20/09	74.00				6
780031	564846	PEARL	RUBY	A	01/22/09		01/22/09	110.00				6
135498	79645	DRAKE	RAKE	F	01/26/09		01/23/09	8.00				2

```
INS CO# 3 BCBSM          PHONE # 800 482 5141       TOTAL    CURRENT   31-60    61-90   OVER 90
                          8 CLAIMS TOTALING        608.00     266.00    0.00    74.00    268.00
```

Date	Patient Name	Claim Number	3rd Party Payer	Amount Billed	Date Paid	Paid by Payer	Remainder	Action
3/15/09	Arnold, James	819211	Advance Insurance 123 Action Ave. Regalstown, MD 23216	$640.00	4/21/09	$600.00	$40.00	$40.00 coinsurance billed to patient
3/16/09	Breznick, Alisa	819230	Singular Insurance Company 10 Park Place Westchester, WA 67511	$178.00				
3/16/09	Milton, Alex	819231	Protection United 244 East End Ave. Dayton, OH 34421	$92.00	4/27/09	$0.00	$92.00	Rejection on being reviewed

018500 HOSP09715

STATEMENT

PAYMENTS MADE AFTER 04/08/2007 WILL APPEAR ON NEXT STATEMENT
QUESTIONS REGARDING THIS INVOICE CAN BE DIRECTED TO THE OFFICE
BETWEEN 1:00PM AND 4:00PM DAILY

ADDRESS SERVICE REQUESTED

| OFFICE PHONE NUMBER | CLOSING DATE 05/04/07 | YOUR ACCOUNT NUMBER | PAGE NO. 01 | PATIENT BALANCE 168.12 |

NOTE: Charges and payments not appearing on this statement will appear on next month's statement.

PLEASE RETURN THIS PORTION WITH PAYMENT

CHARGES APPEARING ON THIS STATEMENT ARE NOT INCLUDED ON ANY HOSPITAL BILL OR STATEMENT

DATE	PROVIDER NAME	EXPLANATION OF ACTIVITY	PATIENT NAME	CHARGES AND DEBITS	PAYMENTS AND CREDITS
072905		INITIAL INPTN CONSULT COMP HISTORY AN		365.00	
073005		FOLLOW CONSULT		250.00	
060205		MEDICARE # 11545 Filed			
092605		PAYMENT MEDICARE c# 115451			-291.17
092605		WRITE-OFF MEDICARE c# 115451			-251.04
092605		Co-ins 72.79			
080105		FOLLOW UP CONSULTATION INPT		720.00	
060205		MEDICARE # 11546 Filed			
092605		PAYMENT MEDICARE c# 115461			-319.68
092605		WRITE-OFF MEDICARE c# 115461			-320.40
092605		Co-ins 79.92			
080905		HOSPITAL DISCHARGE MANAGEMENT 30 MINU		100.00	
060205		MEDICARE # 11547 Filed			
092605		PAYMENT MEDICARE c# 115471			-61.64
092605		WRITE-OFF MEDICARE c# 115471			-22.95
092605		Co-ins 15.41			

STATEMENT CLOSING DATE: 05/04/07   PLEASE INDICATE YOUR ACCOUNT NUMBER WHEN CALLING OUR OFFICE:

CURRENT	30-60 DAYS	60-90 DAYS	> 90 DAYS	TOTAL	INS PENDING	PATIENT BALANCE PAY THIS AMOUNT
			168.12	168.12	0.00	168.12

SEND INQUIRIES TO:

MIDWEST ALLIANCE PLAN

Remittance Advice

Vendor: Marvin Klein MD
515 Somerset
Troy, MI 48098

Vendor ID: P14589
Tax ID #: 382014410
Check Date: 8/25/xxxx
Check Amt:

Provider Number: 14589   Provider Name: Marvin Klein, M.D.

Line Nbr	Reason Code	Status	QTY	Service Date	Rev/Proc Modifier Code	Billed Amt	Contractual Adjustment	Allowed Amt	Copay Amt	Coins Amt	Deductible Amt	Withhold Amt	Paid Amt
Member Name: Harvey Klein				Claim Number Case # 3		Member ID 322457149		HAP Number: 235678-01					
1	PAL04	P	1	07/13/xxxx	10060	$100.00		$95.00				$9.50	$85.50
Member Name: Harvey Klein				Claim Number G1-3		Member ID 322457149		HAP Number: 235678-01					
1	PAL 04	P	1	07/29/xxxx	99212	$45.00		$40.50	$10.00			$4.05	$26.45
Vendor Totals	Nbr of Claims 2					$145.00		$135.50	$10.00			$13.55	$111.95

If you have any questions, please contact Claims investigation and Assessment at 248 443 4400
or 888 260 7003 outside Metro Detroit Area.

Status Legend: P- Payable, H- Held, D – Denied, I- Informational, IP in Process, C- Capitated, A-Adjusted, N- No check

REASON CODE LEGEND

CODE	DESCRIPTION
PAL 04	FEE SCHEDULE – REIMBURSED AT FEE

Aetna US Health Care
PO Box 2559
Fort Wayne IN 46801

EXPLANATION OF BENEFITS
PLEASE RETAIN FOR FUTURE REFERENCE

Date Printed – 9/10/xxxx
Tax ID #: 383214567
Check #: 678598234
Check Amt: $ 35.47

Nigel Brown MD
515 Somerset
Troy, MI 48098

Notes: The benefits listed below reflect your portion of this payment.

Patient Name: Melody Drew Patient Acct #: 351641 ID# 06869-5
Member ID # 221960711
Relation: Child Member: Harry

Service Dates	CPT Codes	PL	NUM SVC	Submitted Charges	Copay Amount	Not Payable	See Remarks	Deduct	Co-Ins	Patient Responsible	Payable Amount
08/01/xx	99212	11	1	$75.00	$25.00	$14.53	893			$39.53	$35.47
TOTALS				$75.00	$25.00	$14.53				$39.53	$35.47

Remark Code 893: Not authorized by Primary Care Physician – reduced reimbursement

For Questions regarding this claim Call 888-6979356 For Assistance. Please use ID number for reference to this claim	Total Patient Responsibility	$39.53

TCF Bank
56624 Highland Rd
Waterford MI 48327

Check #: 678598234

9/10/xxxx

PAY TWENTY & NO/100***

******* $20.00

TO THE ODER OF:
NIGEL BROWN MD
515 SOMERSET
TROY MI 48098

NICHOLAS JONES

Sun Valley PPO
PO Box 16750
Lansing MI 48275

EXPLANATION OF BENEFITS
PLEASE RETAIN FOR FUTURE REFERENCE

Date Printed – 8/25/xxxx
Tax ID #: 382014410
Check #: 3567895234
Check Amt: $

Derek Shepherd MD
186 Maple Ave
Livonia MI 48476

Notes: The benefits listed below reflect your portion of this payment.

Patient Name: Melody Duncan
Patient Acct #: 25631   Patient ID# 268631
Member ID # 977653741
Relation: Spouse   Member: Mark

Service Dates	CPT Codes	PL	NUM SVC	Submitted Charges	Copay Amount	Not Payable	See Remarks	Deduct	Co-Ins	Patient Resp	Payable Amount
08/01/xx	99203	11	1	$115.00	$25.00	$19.44	345			$25.00	$70.56
08/01/xx	93000	11	1	$ 55.00		$ 29.69	345				$25.31
TOTALS				**$170.00**	**$25.00**	**$49.13**				**$25.00**	**$95.87**

Remark Code 345: Contractual write off as a participating physician.

For Questions regarding this claim Call 888-6979356 For Assistance. Please use ID number for reference to this claim	Total Patient Responsibility	$25.00

TCF Bank   Check #: 3567895234
56624 Highland Rd
Waterford MI 48327   8/25/xxxx

PAY FORTY FIVE AND NO/100**   ******** $95.87

TO THE ODER OF:
DEREK SHEPHERD MD
186 MAPLE AVE
LIVONIA MI 48476

Nicholas Jones

Sun Valley PPO
PO Box 16750
Lansing MI 48275

EXPLANATION OF BENEFITS
PLEASE RETAIN FOR FUTURE REFERENCE

Date Printed – 8/25/xxxx
Tax ID #: 382014410
Check #: 3567895234
Check Amt: $ 30.00

Marvin Klein MD
515 Somerset
Troy, MI 48098

Notes: The benefits listed below reflect your portion of this payment.

Patient Name: Jose Martino
Patient Acct #: 25871   Patient ID# 2145556
Member ID # 998741368
Relation: Self   Member: Jose

Service Dates	CPT Codes	PL	NUM SVC	Submitted Charges	Copay Amount	Not Payable	See Remarks	Deduct	Co-Ins	Patient Resp	Payable Amount
07/13/xx	99202	11	1	$115.00		$115.00	231	$115.00		$115.00	$30.00
07/13/xx	93000	11	1	$ 55.00		$ 25.00	231	$ 25.00		$ 25.00	
TOTALS				$170.00		$140.00		$140.00		$140.00	$30.00

Remark Code 231: Provider not in network. Patient's Responsibility

For Questions regarding this claim Call 888-6979356 For Assistance. Please use ID number for reference to this claim	Total Patient Responsibility	$140.00

TCF Bank
56624 Highland Rd
Waterford MI 48327

Check #: 3567895234

8/25/xxxx

PAY Forty five and no/100***

******* $30.00

TO THE ODER OF:
MARVIN KLEIN MD
515 SOMERSET
TROY MI 48098

Nicholas Jones

174

Coding and Billing Audit Form

A. CLAIM INFORMATION

Patient Name: _____   Provider Name: _____

Medical Record # _____   Invoice # _____

Place of Service _____   Type of Service _____

Date of Service _____

WAS THIS ICD-9 CODE CORRECT? YES   NO

ICD-9 Code Billed _____   Corrected ICD-9 Code _____

WAS THE AMOUNT CHARGED CORRECT? YES   NO

Charge Amount _____   Corrected Charge Amount _____

B. REASON(S) FOR REFUND (indicate all that apply)

- **Incorrect of Missing Modifier (If the modifier is payment related)**
- **Incorrect OASIS Code**
- **Incorrect ICD-9 Code (If correct ICD-9 code results in a non-reimbursable service)**
- **Incorrect Place of Service (If correct POS results in a lower or non-reimbursable service)**
- **Duplicate Reimbursement (same charge submitted more than once)**
- **Insufficient documentation for level billed (MUST indicate reason)**

_____

C. ADDITIONAL INFORMATION/COMMENTS/STEPS TO IMPROVE COMPLIANCE _____

D. SIGNATURES/AUTHORIZATIONS

Auditor	Telephone	Date
Compliance Officer	Telephone	Date

Documentation of Patient Services Audit Form

Patient Name: _____ Physician: _____

Medical Record # _____ Invoice # _____

Place of Service: _____ Date of Service _____

(ICD-9 Code) _____ Type of Service _____

Auditor's Name and Telephone Number _____

Compliance Officer's Name and Telephone Number _____

Is the documentation in the patient's chart sufficient? _____ Yes _____ No

Does the documentation support the billing level? _____ Yes _____ No

Is the patient chart in Compliance with our policies? _____ Yes _____ No

If the answer to any of the above questions was no, complete the following.

Non-Compliance resulted from: _____
_____
_____

People Contacted: _____
_____
_____

What was discussed? _____
_____
_____

Steps taken to correct this now and in the future: _____
_____
_____
_____
_____
_____
_____

Medicare/Medicaid Complaint and Resolution Form

Name of person bringing the issue to our attention _____

Address _____

City/State/Zip _____

Phone _____ Fax _____ e-mail _____

Physician(s) involved _____

Medical Record # and Invoice # _____

Date and Place of Service: _____

Level of Service Coded: (CPT Code) _____

Type of Service _____

Name of employee completing this form _____

Address _____

City/State/Zip _____

Date issue first brought to our attention _____

Employee Contacted _____

By phone, in person, other _____

Was the person referred to someone else? Y N. If yes, Name of employee _____

What did the person say: _____

_____

_____

What was the person told: _____

_____

_____

What was done to resolve this issue: _____

_____